Elite • 44

Security Forces in Northern Ireland 1969–92

Tim Ripley • Illustrated by Mike Chappell

Consultant editor Martin Windrow

First published in Great Britain in 1993 by Osprey Publishing,
Midland House, West Way, Botley, Oxford OX2 0PH, UK
44-02 23rd St, Suite 219, Long Island City, NY 11101, USA
Email: info@ospreypublishing.com

Osprey Publishing is part of the Osprey Group.

Transferred to digital print on demand 2011

First published 1993
4th impression 2008

Printed and bound by PrintOnDemand-Worldwide.com, Peterborough, UK

A CIP catalogue record for this book is available from the British Library

ISBN: 978 1 85532 278 3

Filmset in Great Britain

Acknowledgements and author's note

The author wishes to thank the following organizations for their help in the preparation of this volume:
Information Office, Royal Ulster Constabulary, Belfast; Army Information Services, Headquarters Northern Ireland, Lisburn;
Director of Public Relations (Army), Ministry of Defence, London; Public Information Office, 42 (North West) Infantry Brigade,
Preston; Parachute Regiment Museum, Aldershot; Royal Marines Museum, Southsea; Irish Defence Forces; 1st, 2nd and
3rd Battalions, The Parachute Regiment; Military Scene/Bob Morrison. Thanks are also extended to numerous British Army
officers and soldiers who have to remain nameless.
   The views expressed are entirely those of the author and do not represent those of the British Ministry of Defence,
Northern Ireland Office, Royal Ulster Constabulary or Irish Defence Forces.

Note on British Army unit designations

In the text full unit titles are used (i.e. 1st Battalion, The Parachute Regiment) but in picture captions abbreviated titles are used
to save space. These follow the official British Army practice: e.g. the 1st Battalion, The Parachute Regiment, becomes 1 PARA
and the 3rd (Country Down) Battalion, The Ulster Defence Regiment, becomes 3 UDR. The system is self-explanatory, but for
those wishing further information on the subject Osprey's *British Army in the 1980s* (Elite 14) by Mike Chappell is recommended.

The Woodland Trust

Osprey Publishing is supporting the Woodland Trust, the UK's leading woodland conservation charity, by funding the
dedication of trees.

www.ospreypublishing.com

A COMMUNITY IN CONFLICT 1969–1992

For the past 23 years Northern Ireland has been ravaged by inter-communal strife which has left more than 3,000 people dead and over 22,000 injured. The politics of what are known in Northern Ireland as 'the Troubles' are complex, and largely incomprehensible to those not born in the province. Religious bigotry, police brutality, blood feuds stretching back centuries, social and economic deprivation all came to a head in the summer of 1969. Northern Ireland was engulfed in a virtual civil war, with inter-communal riots raging in its two main cities, Belfast and Londonderry. To restore order British Regular Army troops were deployed onto the streets of those two cities. They have been there ever since; and it looks highly likely that the Army will remain deployed operationally in Northern Ireland for the foreseeable future.

The conflict in Northern Ireland is unlike any other campaign conducted by the British Army this century. There have been no set-piece battles, no decisive victories or crushing defeats; just a grinding, relentless series of small scale operations in response to riots, bombings, sectarian murders and terrorist ambushes. It is therefore a difficult task to telescope the events of the past 23 years into this small book. By concentrating on the 'broad brush' approach to events the author hopes to provide the reader with a general guide to the part played by the Security Forces in the Northern Ireland 'Troubles' since 1969.

This book aims to describe how the British Security Forces — the British Regular Army, Ulster Defence Regiment (UDR) and the Royal Ulster Constabulary (RUC) — supported by the Irish Security Forces — the Irish Defence Forces and *Garda Siochana* (Irish Police) — have fought an increasingly sophisticated campaign against terrorists drawn from both Catholic and Protestant communities. An overview of the most important events of the past 23 years is provided as a basic guide to the ebbs and flows of 'the Troubles'. Individual sections then profile the operations, tactics, uniforms and equipment of the British and Irish Security Forces. The main terrorist groups and their *modi operandi* are also examined. For obvious reasons many details of Security Force activities have been omitted to protect on-going operations and the personal safety of members of the Security Forces.

Civil Disorder

Northern Ireland's present civil strife burst into life in the summer of 1969. The trail of events that led to this out-

An officer (left) and an SNCO of 45 Commando in 1971. The officer has a respirator case, a 9mm Browning holster and a Webley-Schermuly flare pistol (used for firing CS gas grenades) holster on his web belt. The two weapons are secured by lanyards. Both men have M1952 flak jackets. (Royal Marines Museum)

Paratroopers received warm welcomes when they first deployed to Northern Ireland, with local people providing cups of tea. The so-called 'Honeymoon period' did not last long. (Airborne Forces Museum)

break of communal violence stretches back to the partition of Ireland after the First World War. As part of a deal between the British Government and the newly independent Irish Republic, the counties of Antrim, Armagh, Down, Fermanagh, Londonderry and Tyrone (normally known collectively to the dominant Protestant majority as Ulster, and to the Catholic/Republican minority as 'the Six Counties') were allowed to remain as part of the United Kingdom in return for a British withdrawal from the remainder of Ireland. A Northern Ireland government was set up by the British, with its own parliament at Stormont. The province's Protestant or Unionist Population (the term refers to their support for the union with the United Kingdom) used their majority of seats in the Stormont parliament and local councils to protect their economic and political privileges at the expense of Northern Ireland's Roman Catholic minority; for despite the partition of the island, a sizeable Roman Catholic population remained in the Six Counties of Ulster alongside the large Protestant majority, and today represents perhaps half a million of the total population of one and half million. Widespread discrimination in politics, employment, education and other areas by the Unionist regime only served to further alienate the Catholics, who generally looked to the Catholic Irish Republic as their protector.

By the late 1960s Northern Ireland's Catholics started to articulate their grievances in a non-violent civil rights movement, which staged demonstrations and other protests to highlight the injustice of the Stormont regime. Increasingly these demonstrations resulted in violence as the Royal Ulster Constabulary and their 'B Special' auxiliaries over-reacted. In summer 1969 the situation was getting out of hand and the RUC began losing control of the streets. Protestants and Catholics formed vigilante groups to protect their neighbourhoods. Firearms began to appear in large numbers. Inter-communal rioting was rife. Protestants saw the civil rights movement as a threat to their position and, ultimately, as an attempt to force them into the Irish Republic. The Irish Government prepared refugee camps in the border region, and the British Government started to consider the deployment of troops to keep the two communities apart.

At 5 p.m. on 14 August 1969 the 1st Battalion, The Prince of Wales Own Regiment deployed in the Catholic Bogside area of Londonderry. In less than a month 6,000 troops were on the streets of Belfast and Londonderry, keeping the Catholics and Protestants from slaughtering each other. This was the beginning of the so-called 'honeymoon' period when Catholics feted the troops as their protectors. It was not to last. The following summer, as violence flared again, the British Army cracked down hard on inter-communal violence in Belfast, carrying out arms searches in the Catholic Falls Road area and imposing a curfew. A new breakaway Catholic 'paramilitary' group (the local euphemism for terrorists, of both communities) called the Provisional Irish Republican Army (PIRA) used this as a pretext for launching attacks on British troops. They hoped to make the province ungovernable and hence to force the British to withdraw, leaving Northern Ireland in their hands. Initially this tactic was undoubtedly effective. In 1971 there were 1,756 shooting incidents, and 10,628 the following year, the majority being the responsibility of the PIRA.

Within months the Royal Ulster Constabulary was on the verge of collapse and the Stormont government was tottering on the brink. August 1971 saw the introduction of internment without trial of suspected terrorists and their activist sympathisers; but it failed to halt the PIRA offensive and, by its relatively indiscriminate application, only served to further discredit the Stormont government. A civil rights demonstration in Londonderry on 30 January 1972 ('Bloody Sunday') ended with 13 civilians being shot dead by soldiers of the 1st Battalion, The Parachute Regiment. Catholics in Northern Ireland and the Irish Republic were outraged both by the deaths and by a judicial inquiry that officially exonerated the paratroopers of wrongdoing — a finding now widely acknowledged as mistaken, not least by soldiers who were involved. The British Embassy in Dublin was burned to the ground, and attacks on troops in Northern Ireland became even more intense. In March 1972 the British Government gave up trying to prod the reluctant Stormont regime into reforming itself and took over control of security policy in the province. The Unionist government at Stormont resigned, and direct rule was established from Westminster. In an attempt to find a solution the Northern Ireland Secretary of State, William Whitelaw, invited six Republican activist leaders, including Gerry Adams, to a secret meeting in London during July. The talks failed; and two days later 12,000 troops were sent into action to re-occupy so-called 'No-Go' areas of Belfast and Londonderry during Operation 'Motorman'. The size of the operation surprised the PIRA defenders and little resistance was offered.

British units now started to dominate Catholic areas

Christmas shopping in Belfast, December 1975. Serving with 45 Cdo Royal Marines, the man in the Denison smock is a Royal Navy Commando, probably a medic or photographer. (Royal Marines Museum)

with heavy patrolling and widespread checkpoints. Soon the PIRA was forced onto the defensive. Car bombs became their favourite urban tactic, while PIRA cells in the border areas started to make life very difficult for British troops.

A move by the British Government in 1974 to set up a power-sharing executive with representatives from both communities generated a Unionist backlash. A general strike and campaign of intimidation called by the extreme Protestant Ulster Workers Council paralysed Northern Ireland. Misleadingly, Protestant extremists described themselves as 'Loyalist' despite their attacks on the Security Forces. The British Army could not cope, and the executive collapsed.

The Way Ahead

The British Government now dug its heels in and decided to adopt a long-term policy to crush the PIRA and Loyalist

A Ferret armoured car supports an Army patrol during the first days of 'the Troubles'. Note Military Policemen behind the vehicle. (AIS HQ NI)

terrorist groups; a solution to the security situation would be necessary before any political progress could be made. In 1976 a security policy called 'The Way Ahead' was adopted, which saw the RUC and UDR taking a more prominent role, with British Regular Army units only being deployed in 'hard' Republican areas where the local Catholic population openly support the PIRA and its political wing, Sinn Fein. Under 'Police Primacy' the RUC would decide the overall security strategy and then assign military units to achieve specific tasks. Internment was discontinued, and arrested terrorist suspects were now to be treated like common criminals.

The RUC and UDR received additional resources to enable them to acquire modern weapons and equipment. Increasing emphasis was put on improving the quality of their training at all levels. RUC pay was increased to attract younger, more motivated recruits, and the UDR formed permanent duty units to take over much of the work from less well trained part-time units. In the British Army a more professional approach was adopted to preparing units for Northern Ireland duty, with the establishment of permanent training units. A wide range of specialist tactical drills were developed to counter PIRA tactics. As a result of all these improvements British Army, police and civilian casualties dropped significantly in the late 1970s and early 1980s, indicating that the Security Forces were making it increasingly difficult for the PIRA and Loyalist terrorist

groups to operate openly as they had done in the early years of 'the Troubles'.

Invisible War

From the late 1970s onwards the conflict in Northern Ireland changed dramatically in character, becoming more a war of intelligence, covert operations, car bombings and back street murders; gone were the days of inter-communal rioting, and large scale gun battles in the streets between troops and terrorists.

The PIRA concentrated on murdering off-duty police and UDR personnel, bombing or mortaring commercial property and Security Forces bases, and attacking British political and military targets in Britain and Continental Europe. The Loyalists made random sectarian killings their speciality, and on occasions the PIRA and other Catholic extremist groups retaliated. Sinn Fein, the PIRA political wing, also staged a major political/propaganda campaign based on opposition to the treatment of arrested PIRA members as criminals; this culminated in the hunger strike campaign of 1980–81. Both the PIRA and Loyalist terrorists became heavily involved in protection rackets as a means of financing their activities. Often the two sides co-operated, for example in 'carving up' Belfast into separate, mutually tolerated areas for criminal exploitation.

In response the Security Forces increasingly orientated their operations towards collecting intelligence on PIRA

and Loyalist terrorists. Covert surveillance and infiltration of PIRA cells was carried out with varying degrees of success. So-called 'super-grasses' or turned terrorists were recruited to work for the Security Forces. 'Executive action' began to be undertaken by plain clothes Security Forces units to catch terrorists red-handed; eight PIRA members were killed in such an ambush at Loughgall in May 1987. Not surprisingly, the Security Forces do not comment on such activities for fear of compromising future operations. This 'no comment' policy also has the effect of undermining morale among terrorist groups: they are kept guessing as to the real reasons for the failure of their operations, and are always looking over their shoulders for traitors within their ranks.

Conventional military and police operations are now orientated to supporting these intelligence and covert operations. Overt patrolling and vehicle checkpoints (VCPs) prevent terrorist groups operating in the open and deter them from moving arms and explosives around. Patrols monitor the movement of terrorist suspects or so-called 'players'. In border areas permanent VCPs and observation towers monitor the movement of suspects across the border with the Irish Republic, and also limit the importation of weaponry. Riot control tactics are now finely tuned to enable public order situations to be brought quickly under control with minimum loss of life and damage to property.

British troops storm past a barricade during the early 1970s. All of them are wearing 1944 pattern helmets and M1952 flak jackets. (AIS HQ NI)

Efforts to strengthen and improve the RUC have largely been successful, with large sections of the Catholic community now accepting the force. The success of the RUC in facing down Loyalist demonstrations opposing the Anglo-Irish Agreement in 1985 won the RUC much praise in the Catholic community.

This agreement between Dublin and London also proved a turning point in security co-operation between the two governments. In 1987, after French customs officers intercepted a ship carrying 150 tons of arms destined for the PIRA, the Irish Security Forces mounted a massive search for arms throughout the Republic.

Continuing Conflict

Over two decades of violence have undoubtedly left their mark on Northern Ireland. The intervention of the British Army in 1969 and through until the mid-1970s put a halt to the most widespread sectarian violence. The rebuilding of the local Security Forces, the RUC and UDR, in the late 1970s allowed the Regular Army to scale down its involvement. By the early 1980s a degree of normality had returned to the province. On a per capita basis, levels of violence were significantly less than those normal in American cities such as New York and Los Angeles.

From media reports it would be easy to gain an impression of Northern Ireland as a war-zone; however, the vast majority of the province's population, both Catholic and Protestant, now go about their business in a peaceful manner and have no involvement with terrorist groups. By 1992 Northern Ireland was undergoing something of an economic renaissance. Only the presence of armed troops and policemen would enable a visitor to Belfast city centre to differentiate it from the commercial centre of any other British city. The Security Forces estimate that through a combination of their overt patrolling and undercover intelligence gathering operations they prevent more than two-thirds of all planned terrorist attacks.

This achievement has been the result of sustained efforts by the Security Forces to defeat terrorism; however, the Security Forces have not been able to totally eradicate the PIRA and its Loyalist counterparts. Each year the level of PIRA activity drops and its support in the Catholic community is gradually reduced; but the terrorists still seem able to bounce back from reverses, mounting 'spectacular' operations to recapture public attention. Security Forces commanders now talk of an 'acceptable level of violence' and a 'war of attrition' to wear down the terrorists.

The continuing failure of Northern Ireland's politicians, along with those in London and Dublin, to reach an accommodation on the future of the province still prevents the final chapter on 'the Troubles' from being closed.

PRINCIPAL TERRORIST GROUPS:

P.I.R.A.

The PIRA was formed in 1970 after a split in the Official Irish Republican Army (OIRA) which had its roots in the guerrilla army which fought the British after the First World War. During the August 1969 riots the Dublin-based Marxist faction of the OIRA proved unwilling and unable to defend the Catholic ghettos of Belfast and Londonderry from Protestant mobs. In response to this inactivity more radical Northern Irish elements of the IRA decided to take matters into their own hands and formed the Provisional IRA. They adopted a radical revolutionary socialist agenda to appeal to underprivileged sections of Northern Ireland's Catholic population; this, however, was couched in romantic nationalist terms in order to se-

cure support from outside Northern Ireland, particularl in North America. Its aim is to force the British to with draw from Northern Ireland as a prelude to overthrowin what it calls the 'collaborator' regime of the Irish Republic A campaign of bombing and murders in Northern Irelan and mainland Britain is intended to force British publi opinion to turn against the British military presence i Northern Ireland through disgust at all things Irish.

Until 1972 the PIRA was closely linked to the com munity defence committees in Catholic ghetto areas. Arm were acquired from a variety of sources and volunteer were trained in their use. A military organisation was set u on conventional lines with so-called 'brigades' and 'batta lions' (of nothing approaching the size suggested by suc terms) responsible for the defence of particular location During the existence of the 'No-Go' areas such as 'Fre Derry' PIRA units operated openly. After Operatio 'Motorman' in July 1972 the PIRA was forced to go under ground to escape the attentions of the Security Forces. A the British Army and RUC re-established their intelli gence gathering operations in Catholic areas during th mid-1970s the PIRA's command structure was decimated with many key personnel ending up behind bars.

In a bid to protect itself from infiltration the PIR adopted a three- to five-man cell structure along classic ter rorist lines. So-called Active Service Units (ASUs) becam strictly compartmentalised with only key commander knowing full details of the organisation. A few specialist became responsible for procuring arms, bomb-making assassinations, mortars, training, intelligence gatherin and 'fund raising' (the latter including bank robberies an protection rackets).

The cell system has been remarkably successful, an while the Security Forces have been able to cause heav damage to the PIRA they have yet to destroy it. The organ isation's strengths and weaknesses were summarised i great detail in a December 1978 report by Brigadier J. M Glover, of the British Defence Intelligence Staff, whic was later leaked to the press: 'Our evidence of the calibre o rank and file terrorists does not support the view that the are merely mindless hooligans drawn from the unemploy able and unemployed. PIRA now trains and uses its mem bers with some care. ... The ASUs are for the most par manned by terrorists tempered by up to ten years of oper ational experience.

'The mature terrorists, including for instance the lead ing bomb makers, are usually sufficiently cunning to avoi arrest. They are continually learning from their mistake and developing their expertise. We can therefore expect t see increasing professionalism and the greater exploitatio of modern technology for terrorist purposes.'

PIRA tactics have become increasingly complex, bu

they are all designed to allow ASU members a high probability of escaping safely. Commanders or 'Godfathers' nominate targets for ASUs, who then pick up their weapons or explosives from secret arms caches. Often teenagers who aspire to PIRA membership are used as couriers or 'dickers' to make last-minute reconnaissance of targets, for example by following Security Force patrols or collecting the car registration numbers of intended murder victims. (In one major attack on a Security Force base more than 50 'dickers' were used.) Training camps are believed to be run in remote parts of the Irish Republic. Promotion through the ranks of the PIRA depends largely on success. Those terrorists who are not very good are quickly caught by the Security Forces, leaving only the most determined and skilful at large.

Brigadier Glover estimated that at that date the PIRA had some 1,700 active members, with hundreds of sympathisers on either side of the Irish border who are willing to provide 'safe houses' between operations. Key PIRA personnel operate entirely underground to escape Security Forces surveillance and receive regular wages from the

The Webley-Schermuly riot gun is one of a number of weapons used by the Security Forces in public order situations to fire plastic bullets. (AIS HQ NI)

Paratroopers debus from a short wheel base Land Rover. The M1952 flak jackets and Denison smocks were common items of kit with Airborne units in the early 1970s. (Airborne Forces Museum)

organisation. The PIRA's multi-million-pound budget is provided from a variety of sources, including donations from sympathisers in the USA, bank robberies and protection rackets in Northern Ireland and the Irish Republic, 'front' companies, and drinking clubs in Northern Ireland. 'Kangaroo courts' and the 'kneecapping' (shooting in the knee at point blank range) of petty criminals in Catholic ghettos help enforce continued support for the PIRA in these areas. Alleged informers receive similar treatment or are summarily murdered — after merciless interrogation.

Over the past 23 years the PIRA has continued to attract a steady stream of volunteers in spite of the heavy arrest and casualty rates suffered by its ASUs. Motivations for joining include sectarian bigotry, the social prestige in Catholic ghettos of being in the PIRA, and romantic Irish nationalism; a proportion of recruits also exhibit psychopathic tendencies. As Security Forces intelligence efforts have increased the PIRA leadership has tried to recruit a special cadre of terrorists who do not have known Republican backgrounds or criminal records, to enable them to operate undetected on the British mainland.

Close links exist with the PIRA's political wing, Sinn Fein, which operates openly. Leading Sinn Fein figures openly proclaim their support for the PIRA and describe the Republican movement's strategy as 'a ballot box in one hand and an Armalite in the other'. Gerry Adams, the former Sinn Fein MP for West Belfast, is widely believed to be one of the founders of the PIRA, although the allegation has never been tested in court. Another top Sinn Fein man, Danny Morrison, was jailed in 1991 for his part in the kidnapping of an RUC informer. The man was rescued by the RUC during a PIRA 'kangaroo court' in which Morrison was sitting in judgement as the PIRA's so-called 'Lord Chief Justice'.

Back in 1978 British intelligence estimated that the

This 1 DERR soldier is armed with an American M16A and is wearing a commercially purchased 'SAS smock'. A number of M16As are issued to units on rural patrol operations. Note the stock of the weapon is secured by a lanyard. (AIS HQ NI)

PIRA had a stock of some 4,000 handguns, machine guns and rifles. This arsenal is now thought to be much larger thanks to a series of massive shipments from Colonel Gaddafi of Libya in the mid-1980s. In the early 1970s a hotchpotch of weapons were used by the PIRA, including old Thompson sub-machine guns. When American support for the PIRA was at its height in the mid to late 1970s Armalites and M60 machine guns were the commonest weapons in their arsenal. The PIRA then spread their arms-buying net to include the Middle East; and soon Eastern Bloc arms started appearing on the streets of Northern Ireland, including RPG-7 rocket launchers, AK-47 assault rifles and quantities of powerful Czech-made Semtex plastic explosive.

In 1987 French customs and police seized the trawler *Eksund* which was found to be loaded with 150 tons of Libyan arms destined for the PIRA. The haul included 50 tons of ammunition, 1,000 AK-47s, 600 grenades, two tons of Semtex, ten 12.7mm heavy machine guns, and 20 SAM-7 heat-seeking anti-aircraft missiles. Four previous shiploads of Libyan weapons, including anti-tank rocket launchers and flamethrowers, are believed to have been

A patrol of 1 CHESHIRE move along a South Armagh road, well spaced to avoid the whole patrol being wiped out if any members of it detonate booby traps. All are wearing DPM pattern waterproof jackets. (AIS HQ NI)

landed in the Irish Republic before the *Eskund* was intercepted. SAM-7s are thought to have been fired at British helicopters in July 1991, but none scored hits.

The PIRA also produces a wide range of its own explosives and weapons, particularly improvised mortars. Agricultural fertiliser is turned into high explosive in a number of underground laboratories for use in car bombs, culvert bombs and car booby traps. Proxy or 'human' bombs containing up to 3,000lbs of explosives are regularly used by the PIRA to destroy Security Forces bases or commercial property; these bombs are driven to their targets by innocent civilians whose families are being held hostage. Heavy civilian casualties usually result from the use of proxy bombs.

Individuals are targeted with under-car booby traps or improvised explosive devices (IEDs) triggered by timers or mercury tilt switches. In rural areas culvert bombs

controlled by command wires or radio are used to attack Security Forces vehicle patrols. A new addition to the PIRA arsenal are bombs activated by camera flashes and photo electric cells. 'Mortars' are a favourite PIRA weapon, and their current versions show a remarkable degree of sophistication. Early versions were simple drainage pipes mounted on the back of flat bed trucks. The latest PIRA mortars are concealed inside vans to allow them to be driven undetected close to their firing points. One of these vans was used to attack the official residence of the British Prime Minister in Downing Street, London, in February 1991. These mortars are usually fired by remote or timed control rather than served by crews in the conventional military manner.

I.N.L.A.

The Irish National Liberation Army (INLA) was once considered to be the most dangerous terrorist group in Northern Ireland thanks to the murderous behaviour of its one-time leader Dominic McGlinchy. Prior to his arrest in 1984 McGlinchy boasted that he had personally killed more than 30 people. An extreme Marxist-Leninist group the INLA was thought never to have mustered more than 50 activists. Its most famous operation was the murder of British MP Airey Neave in the House of Commons car park in 1979.

After McGlinchy's arrest the organisation was racked by a bloody internal power struggle which culminated in many of its leading members being killed in 1987. On occasions the PIRA has even taken action against the INLA when its interests have been threatened. In 1987 the INLA splintered, resulting in the formation of a new grouping called the Irish People's Liberation Organisation (IPLO) which attracted most of the old INLA supporters.

Loyalist Terrorist Groups

In comparison to Republican terrorist groups, their Protestant counterparts have been significantly less well organised or armed. After clashing with British troops on the streets of Belfast in the first years of 'the Troubles' the Loyalists have concentrated their attention on random sectarian killings of innocent Catholics, attacks on alleged PIRA/Sinn Fein personnel, and organised crime.

While officially a legal political organisation prior to its banning in August 1992, the Ulster Defence Association (UDA) is regarded as the largest and best organised Loyalist paramilitary group. It is closely linked with the Ulster Freedom Fighters (UFF), who are blamed for committing some of the most brutal and senseless killings ever seen in Northern Ireland. Random sectarian killings of innocent civilians in response to alleged PIRA attacks on the Protestant community are its trademark. By 1990 the Protestant terrorists were believed to be responsible for 29 per cent of all murders and 10 per cent of explosions in Northern Ireland over the previous 21 years.

The UDA grew out of the vigilante groups set up in 1969 to protect Protestant areas of Belfast and Londonderry. In the mid-1970s, as open sectarian conflict subsided, the UDA leadership turned increasingly to crime as a means of sustaining their hold on their organisations. The UDA set up a string of 'front' companies in Northern Ireland to launder the money collected from its many protection rackets. Throughout the 1970s and 1980s UDA members were regularly convicted for serious terrorist crimes, indicating that it was still in the murder business — if on a smaller scale than the PIRA. It emerged in the late 1980s that the South African government was one of the Loyalists' arms suppliers, the weapons being exchanged for military secrets stolen from the Shorts Bros. aircraft and missile factory in Belfast.

The lack of inclination among the UDA leadership to wholeheartedly take up the struggle against the PIRA led to a number of splinter groups deciding to take matters into their own hands. These included the Red Hand Commandos (RHC) and the Ulster Freedom Fighters (UFF). Another Loyalist paramilitary group, the Ulster Volunteer Force (UVF), was in existence before 1969 and was active throughout the 1970s until 11 of its members, the so-called 'Shankill Butchers', were given a total of 42 life sentences for multiple murders in 1979. It later splintered when the Protestant Action Force became active in the late 1980s and early 1990s.

Until 1991 the UFF/UDA leadership was made up of veterans of the struggles of the early 1970s, and they were considered to be only interested in maintaining their 'gangster boss' lifestyles. The organisation's operations became characterised by sloppiness, and it was easily infiltrated by Security Forces informers at very high levels. During the mid and late 1980s the UDA's chief intelligence officer,

A PIRA mortar. These crude but effective weapons are highly favoured by the PIRA. They have devoted a lot of effort to modifying and improving their designs. (AIS HQ NI)

Brian Nelson, was on the payroll of Army Intelligence. In late 1991 a younger and more aggressive leadership took over control of the UDA/UFF and copied the PIRA cell structure. It then embarked on a series of attacks on what it called 'PIRA/Sinn Fein targets'. The attacks were carried out with a degree of expertise previously not noted among Loyalist groups, and sparked a major outbreak of reprisal killings between the PIRA and the Loyalists. In the first four months of 1992 the UFF murdered 13 people and the PIRA retaliated by murdering 12 people. Not surprisingly, most of the victims were innocent civilians.

Loyalist political leaders have on a number of occasions been speculatively linked to so-called 'Doomsday Organisations' or paramilitary groups intended to defend Northern Ireland's Protestants in the event of a British withdrawal. These shadowy organisations have gone under a variety of names such as the Orange Volunteers (OV) and Loyalist Defence Volunteers (LDV), and the most recent incarnation was the 'Third Force' in 1981: it held a well publicised parade of 15,000 men at Newtownards, but little has been heard of it since then. Although they are reported not to have taken part in any violence Security Forces sources indicate that they have access to considerable quantities of arms.

THE ROYAL ULSTER CONSTABULARY

The RUC's 8,250 regular and 4,500 full-time or part-time reserve personnel are in the forefront of the campaign against terrorism in Northern Ireland. Since the late 1970s the RUC's role has steadily increased, and it now only relies on military escorts to carry out its duties in 'hard' Republican areas such as South Amagh and West Belfast. Senior RUC officers, acting in consultation with British Army commanders, now determine overall security policy and are responsible for the everyday control of security operations throughout Northern Ireland. In addition to making great advances in combating terrorism the RUC has one of the highest detection rates of ordinary crime of any United Kingdom police force. Even with the terrorist situation Northern Ireland's murder rate is only a third of that recorded in New York or other American cities.

Eastern Bloc arms such as these AKM assault rifles were used in increasing *numbers by the PIRA during the 1980s. (AIS HQ NI)*

Back in 1969 the RUC was a totally different force. The civil rights marches and subsequent rioting had stretched the 3,000-strong RUC to breaking point. British Army officers took command of the situation on the ground and RUC policemen took refuge from a hostile population inside fortified police stations. The force had no modern weapons, poor communications and few armoured vehicles. The Army had little confidence in it and consequently tended to sideline the force. Not surprisingly, morale slumped and recruiting suffered accordingly.

In 1974 the Security Forces began the long process of modernising the RUC, which culminated in 1976 with the start of the 'Way Ahead' programme. Under their new Chief Constable Kenneth Newman the RUC were given overall responsibility for security in Northern Ireland; the technical term for the arrangement is 'Police Primacy'. A series of high level committees were set up to co-ordinate police/military operations. At RUC Divisional and Sub-Divisional level joint headquarters were established to ensure smooth co-ordination. At all levels of command Army operations, such as house searches and vehicle checkpoints, would only be undertaken in response to requests from RUC officers.

Newman also set out to improve the RUC to ensure that it would be up to this new and demanding role. Officers of all ranks were rigorously re-trained. Salaries and overtime pay were significantly increased. New equipment was introduced, including armoured Land Rovers; the first of these were called Hotspurs but they have since been superseded by more advanced versions such as the Tangi and Simba. US-made M1 carbines and British Army SLRs were also acquired. Riot training was given to special RUC units to allow the force to take over from the Army in policing public disorder; the first such unit was called the Special Patrol Group. By 1980 each division had formed a highly trained Divisional Mobile Support Unit to deal with riots, demonstrations and paramilitary funerals; they

This battered Series II Land Rover has had a Vehicle Protection Kit (VPK) applied. The 'wire-cutter' post fitted above the passenger door is designed to stop soldiers standing in the rear compartment being decapitated by wire strung between lamp-posts. (Bob Morrison/Military Scene)

After much experimentation with add-on armour kits the British Army started to introduce a purpose designed version of the Land Rover during the mid-1980s called the Armoured Patrol Vehicle (APV). (Bob Morrison/Military Scene)

*Paratroopers from 1 PARA
monitor traffic from an
APV. (1 PARA)*

were provided with riot helmets, body armour, and riot guns firing baton rounds or 'rubber bullets'. Large investments were made in computers and forensic science support to improve the RUC's intelligence gathering capability.

RUC Special Branch received a major boost to allow it to take the leading role in the collection of intelligence on terrorist groups. A special surveillance unit was set up to carry out photographic and electronic intelligence gathering; this unit, called E4A, played a prominent part in the events leading up to the so-called 'Stalker affair'. To provide armed undercover units the Special Branch set up the Headquarters Mobile Support Unit (HMSU) with help from the SAS.

The first major test of the Police Primacy policy came in 1980 when the PIRA mounted its H-Block hunger strike campaign to try to win POW status for its members serving sentences in the Maze Prison south of Belfast. Widespread rioting broke out in West Belfast which was dealt with very professionally by the RUC.

A more serious challenge occurred in July 1985 when in the run-up to the signing of the Anglo-Irish Agreement the RUC successfully confronted Protestant Orangemen trying to stage provocative demonstrations in Catholic areas. When the Agreement was signed in November 1985 the RUC, under the then-Chief Constable Jack Hermon stood firm against attacks by Loyalist extremists; a number of attacks were even mounted on the homes of policemen but the RUC did not break ranks. The following year protests continued against the Agreement, and the RUC even fired rubber bullets at Protestant rioters. Public respect for the RUC on all sides of the community was considerably enhanced by its even-handed response to those provocations.

Another crisis gripped the RUC during this period due to the controversy surrounding the investigation into the killings of six Catholics by the HMSU undercover unit. Amid accusations that the RUC had a 'shoot-to-kill' policy, Greater Manchester Police's Assistant Chief Constable John Stalker was brought in to investigate the killings. His suspension in mysterious circumstances, and a Government decision not to prosecute the officers concerned on the grounds of 'national security' even after irregularities had been found in their evidence during a court case, meant that the matter was never properly resolved.

Today the RUC is highly experienced in the investigation of terrorist crime. Criminal Investigation Department (CID) officers are responsible for bringing criminal prosecutions against terrorist suspects. All shootings and bombings are methodically investigated. Scenes of crime officers, forensic and photographic officers collect evidence that might lead to conviction. As might be expected, a high degree of expertise has been built up concerning the effects of firearms and explosives, although the Royal Army Ordnance Corps also provide help in this latter area. To carry out Province-wide investigations the Serious Crime Squad is on call.

An Anti-Racketeering Squad has been established to stop the flow of funds to terrorist groups from tax evasion, frauds, video piracy, drinking clubs and protection rackets. Investigations into fraud in the construction industry have resulted in many successful prosecutions for offences involving millions of pounds. Gambling and cross-border smuggling are also investigated. Acting on information from the RUC Anti-Racketeering Squad, 1,000 troops and police mounted a massive search operation in Armagh and County Down in May 1990; in a surprise raid, 20 Army and RAF helicopters lifted Security Forces, personnel to 29 locations. A substantial quantity of documents were seized.

The RUC is now expert in what it terms 'Security by Design', or the fortification of its stations. In 1990 eight RUC stations were damaged as a direct result of terrorist attack. Mortars are regularly used, and large car bombs are also a favourite PIRA method of attack; bombs in excess of 2,000lbs of explosive have been used, causing massive damage and large numbers of civilian casualties.

Surveillance and collection of intelligence on terrorist groups is the responsibility of RUC Special Branch. Details of its activities are highly secret but it is known to

Royal Army Medical Corps ambulance units were issued with Saracen APCs in the 1970s to enable them to operate in support of Army units in 'hard' Republican areas. (AIS HQ NI)

In 1973/74 Saracen APCs in Northern Ireland were fitted with anti-rocket mesh, under a programme called Operation 'Kremlin', to protect them from RPG-7 anti-tank rockets being used by the PIRA. (AIS HQ NI)

Right: The premier riot control vehicle for most of the 1970s and 1980s was the 'Flying Pig' which featured hinged mess screens, which could be deployed to protect troops from rioters' bricks and other missiles. (AIS HQ NI)

include the infiltration of agents and informers into the ranks of terrorist groups. Close co-operation is maintained with MI5 and Army Intelligence, who carry out similar types of operations.

Day-to-day liaison with the Army is carried out at joint military/police headquarters, usually at battalion/police division and company/sub-division level. Boundaries of police and military areas of responsibility are also similar to ease command and control problems. Action committees are established at all levels of military/police command to set policy objectives, to select tasks for the police and military units, and to assess the progress of on-going operations. These range from the Province Executive Committee headed by the RUC Deputy Chief Constable and including the Army Commander of Land Forces, through to Regional Action Committees at Brigade level, Divisional Action Committees at Battalion level, and Sub-Division Action Committees at Company level.

Where possible, RUC officers accompany Army patrols to fulfil the requirements of 'Police Primacy'. It is the ultimate aim of the RUC for it to be able to police all of Northern Ireland without military support. During major public order situations such as paramilitary demonstrations or funerals the Army now keeps well in the background and leaves direct contact with demonstrators to the RUC. Army patrols are usually in reserve in case they are needed. Aerial surveillance is provided by Army Air Corps helicopters fitted with Heli-Teli equipment to relay video images back to the incident control point.

Because RUC officers and reservists live in the community they have often been the target of terrorist murder squads; many officers have been murdered in their homes or have had their cars booby-trapped. By the end of 1991 some 284 policemen had been killed and 6,800 injured. Not surprisingly, RUC personnel are under considerable stress; and few officers have not had close colleagues killed or maimed in the course of their duties. This problem was highlighted in February 1992 when an RUC officer was so distressed at the death of a colleague that he staged a lone attack on the Sinn Fein headquarters in West Belfast, killing three people before turning his weapon on himself.

While the RUC has to concentrate a great deal of time and resources on countering terrorism it also has to carry out all the other activities expected of a police force, such as attending road traffic accidents, investigating burglaries and other petty crime, running crime prevention courses, and issuing parking tickets. ... It is a great tribute to the professionalism of the RUC that it continues to carry out such duties in much the same way as police forces anywhere else in the world.

THE BRITISH ARMY

When British Regular Army troops moved into Londonderry's Bogside district in August 1969 after three days of violent inter-communal rioting, few of those soldiers would have expected the Army to still be deployed operationally on the streets of Northern Ireland 23 years later. Up to 1992 the Army has suffered more than 400 fatal

casualties, and almost 4,700 service personnel have been injured.

By the early 1980s the Army had perfected its anti-terrorist tactics procedures and equipment to such an extent that it is considered to be one of the world's leading exponents of counter-insurgency operations. Officers of the new Russian Security Forces have even visited Northern Ireland to learn how to deal with civil unrest.

Things were very different in 1969. While British troops had plenty of experience in dealing with guerrilla warfare in former colonies, the situation in Northern Ireland was unprecedented. Two communities sharing a part of Britain seemed intent on tearing each other apart. The local police and political structures had collapsed, or were siding with one faction against the other. Few British soldiers or politicians had any idea about how to deal with the sectarian violence. In those first days the 3,000 troops on the streets of Belfast and Londonderry could do little but try to position themselves between opposing mobs in the hope that their presence would keep the two sides at a safe distance. Sometimes it worked, and sometimes it did not. Army commanders often found that public services had collapsed in many areas and had to deal with a whole range of problems, such as providing housing and food for refugees, and even escorting postmen.

Soldiers had little protection against the bricks and firebombs that were regularly hurled at them. A few rudimentary riot shields were soon made available, along with old wheeled GKN Sankey FV-1611 armoured personnel carriers popularly called 'Pigs'. These had previously been intended for the scrapyard, but were called back into service when the British Government stopped the Army deploying its then new FV432 tracked APCs on the grounds that tracked vehicles were too provocative — they conjured up images of the 1968 Soviet invasion of Czecho-slovakia. The only non-lethal riot control weapon available was CS gas (a form of tear gas), and this was far from ideal. As the number of troops in Northern Ireland spiralled dozens of buildings were commandeered as Army bases. Old mills, industrial premises, hotels and police stations were turned into temporary barracks. Living conditions were extremely primitive, but the troops had little time to savour them: they were too busy out on the streets.

When the PIRA started its offensive the Army responded by aggressively patrolling Catholic areas of Belfast and Londonderry to try to nip the terrorist campaign in the bud. Large scale house searches were made to find weapons caches, and curfews were imposed. With the imposition of internment without trial in 1971 hundreds of PIRA suspects were arrested and held in prison camps. Much of the intelligence provided by the RUC proved to be faulty, and most of the PIRA leadership escaped the round-up. British units then set up their own under-cover squads in an attempt to gain intelligence on their elusive PIRA opponents. These measures produced few results, and violence escalated to the extent that there were more than 10,000 shooting incidents in 1972 compared to only 1,756 the year before. Fire-fights between PIRA and Army units were common, and for good measure the Loyalists often took pot-shots at Army patrols. PIRA gunmen operated openly in the so-called 'No-Go' areas of Belfast and Londonderry.

The struggle between the PIRA and the Army came to a head in summer 1972. In the early hours of 31 July some 12,000 of the 21,000 British troops in Northern Ireland

Versions of the Saxon wheeled APC, modified for internal security work, are to replace the 'Pig' on the streets of Northern Ireland during the 1990s. (Tim Ripley)

were sent into action against the Catholic 'No-Go' areas. Five infantry battalions — supported by Centurion AVRE bulldozer tanks of 26 Armoured Engineer Squadron, RE, landed from HMS *Fearless* — moved into the Bogside and Creggan areas of Londonderry. In West Belfast 11 infantry battalions were sent into action. The PIRA were taken completely by surprise and minimal resistance was encountered; a gunman and a petrol-bomber shot dead in Londonderry were the only casualties. Army units now set about dominating the urban areas of Northern Ireland. Heavy patrolling kept PIRA gunmen and bombers underground. A major effort was put into gathering intelligence, and a census was made of every household to build up a complete picture of likely PIRA supporters. In 1973 the number of shootings halved, and the following year it almost halved again. Something approaching 'normality' was slowly returning to Northern Ireland.

The Long Haul

With the formulation of the 'Way Ahead' strategy in the mid-1970s the Army began to settle in for the long haul, with large scale investments in new equipment, buildings and training. Troop levels were gradually scaled down as the RUC was built up and took over responsibility for policing almost all of Northern Ireland. By 1980 only some 11,000 Regular British Army troops remained in Northern Ireland — about half the number deployed in 1972. These numbers have largely remained constant throughout the 1980s and into the 1990s, although on a number of occasions additional troops have been deployed to deal with particular situations. In 1985 the force strength went below the 10,000 level for the first time since the 1960s, to some 9,000 Regular Army soldiers; but two extra battalions

(1,200 men) soon had to be deployed to protect Security Forces bases from a PIRA mortar campaign.

Army operations and deployments took on a more routine flavour. In 1981 the majority of units in Northern Ireland were serving 18-month or two-year fixed tours as resident or garrison units; these included five infantry battalions, an armoured reconnaissance regiment, three engineer squadrons, two Army Air Corps (AAC) squadrons, and numerous support units such as Royal Army Ordnance (RAOC), Explosive Ordnance Disposal (EOD) or bomb-disposal teams.

Seven battalion-sized units a year were deployed on four-month Operation 'Banner' or *roulement* ('rolling') tours, patrolling 'hard' Republican areas. Royal Air Force helicopters were deployed to support Army operations. An RAF Regiment guard force protected Aldergrove International Airport, Belfast, during the first years of 'the Troubles' but was withdrawn in the early 1980s.

By 1992 the mix of units had slightly altered; troop numbers stood at 10,500 Regular Army, 6,000 UDR, 1,000 RAF and 250 Royal Navy. The Regular Army contribution consisted of six resident battalions serving two-and-a-half-year tours, and at any one time four roulement battalions serving in the province on six-month tours. In early 1992 three additional roulement units were temporarily deployed to deal with a major PIRA bombing campaign against Belfast city centre.

Army Headquarters in Northern Ireland is based at Thiepval Barracks in Lisburn, about ten miles south of Belfast. The General Officer Commanding Northern Ireland, normally a lieutenant-general, commands all servicemen in the province. Below him the Commander Land Forces, a major-general, controls all the day-to-day military operations necessary to enable the RUC to carry out its duties. The next step down the military chain of command is to the three Army brigades which are responsible for specific geographic areas.

Covering the south-eastern and central portion of Northern Ireland, which stretches from Strangford Lough across the border area of South Armagh and into mid-Tyrone, is 3 Infantry Brigade with headquarters in the town of Armagh. The brigade is responsible for the notorious 'Bandit Country' of South Armagh. In the late 1980s a series of sixteen 20 metre high observation towers were constructed along the Brigade's 50-mile section of border with the Irish Republic, overlooking key crossing points and intended to interdict the movement of arms, ammunition and explosives into Northern Ireland. The observation towers and permanent vehicle checkpoints (PVCPs) are interlinked with a programme of closing minor border roads to channel the movement of border traffic through the PVCPs, making it easier for the Security Forces to monitor. Most of the brigade's bases in the border region are resupplied by helicopter because of the danger to vehicles from land mines and improvised explosive devices (IEDs). The brigade's area contains the four Divisions of the RUCs South Region and the Armagh Roulement Battalion.

The counties of Fermanagh, western Tyrone, Londonderry and Antrim are the responsibility of 8 Infantry Brigade, which has its headquarters in the city of Londonderry. Resident battalions are based in the city, at nearby Ballykelly and Omagh; roulement units are usually based in Fermanagh. Four Divisions of the RUC's North Region are covered by the brigade. Some 13 PVCPs are maintained by the brigade along its 150-mile section of border with the Republic. The PVCPs have automatic barriers and soldiers talk to drivers through an intercom system at night. Two PVCPs were closed in March 1991 after Coshquin checkpoint was devastated by a PIRA 'human bomb' attack in October 1990; five soldiers and a civilian were killed after the latter's family were held hostage while he was forced to drive a vehicle packed with explosives into the checkpoint. To provide the PCVPs with extra protection .50 cal. Browning heavy machine guns and French-made Luchaire Close Light Assault Weapons (CLAW) were issued to units in Northern Ireland; the 40mm CLAW rocket grenades have HEAT warheads and are fired from standard SA-80 rifles.

From its headquarters at Lisburn 39 Infantry Brigade looks after the Greater Belfast area. This includes sensitive locations such as the Maze Prison (which contains the largest concentration of PIRA personnel in Northern

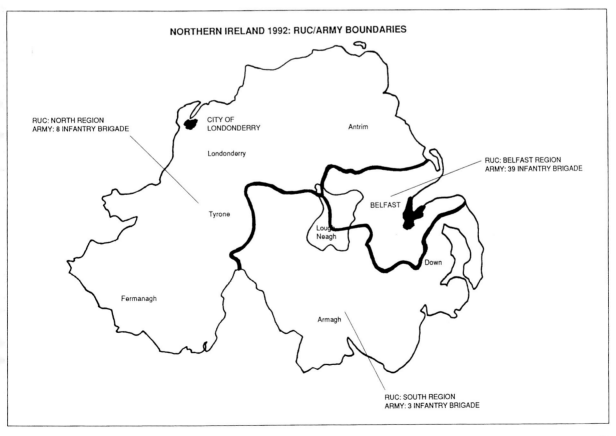

NORTHERN IRELAND 1992: RUC/ARMY BOUNDARIES

RUC: NORTH REGION
ARMY: 8 INFANTRY BRIGADE

CITY OF LONDONDERRY

Antrim

Londonderry

RUC: BELFAST REGION
ARMY: 39 INFANTRY BRIGADE

BELFAST

Tyrone

Lough Neagh

Down

Fermanagh

Armagh

RUC: SOUTH REGION
ARMY: 3 INFANTRY BRIGADE

Ireland), Aldergrove International Airport and the 'hard' Republican areas of West Belfast. That area is usually patrolled by the Belfast Roulement Battalion, while other parts of the city are the responsibility of resident battalions quartered at Hollywood and Aldergrove. The Maze is usually guarded by a company sized perimeter guard force, termed the Prison Guard Force, drawn from non-infantry units such as the Royal Signals or Royal Artillery.

An infantry Spearhead Battalion is kept on standby in mainland Britain for deployment to Northern Ireland should a crisis develop requiring extra manpower. It is usually flown into the province by RAF transport aircraft; the battalion's sub-units are then flown to rural bases by RAF Chinook helicopters. Units deployed to Northern Ireland at short notice have usually just returned from the province after resident or roulement tours; this ensures that they are fully prepared for operations as soon as they arrive.

The brunt of the British Army's campaign in Northern Ireland has fallen on its infantry battalions. Not surprisingly, a high degree of expertise has been built up, and tours in the province now hold few surprises for the British infantryman.

Tours

In general terms, RUC/Army operations in Northern Ireland have three main aims: the first is to reassure the public by being seen to be out on streets actively combating terrorist activity. Secondly, patrols and vehicle checkpoints are designed to introduce doubt and uncertainty into ter-

rorist planning, and to deter terrorists from carrying out attacks because of the risks of being caught or killed. Finally, terrorist activities are to be reduced by arresting terrorist suspects and seizing their weapons, ammunition and explosives.

Many Army operations involve providing protection and support to enable the RUC to carry out its duties. This is termed military escort ('Mike-Echo') duty, and includes a wide range of activities from protecting police officers issuing summonses to putting in cordons to protect large police operations. Specialist units such as EOD and Army Air Corps also support the RUC.

For units deployed to Northern Ireland for resident tours the routine is very different from those on roulement tours. Resident units are based in garrisons in largely peaceful Protestant areas; these include married quarters, so soldiers' families usually accompany the unit during its tour.

Although specifics vary from unit to unit, it is often the case that companies are used in cycle to fulfil the battalion's tasks: e.g. one company will be needed to guard the garrison, others will be deployed away from base as Brigade Operations Companies and some elements will be on leave. Battalions rarely operate as formed units, with companies and sub-units being tasked to support a number of Tactical Area of Responsibility (TAOR) Headquarters. Except for direct operational tasks life for soldiers of resident units is very similar to garrison life in Britain or Germany.

Roulement units have a very different lifestyle. They

A typical scene inside a Security Forces base, 1992. (1 PARA)

live in severely cramped Security Forces bases in West Belfast or along the border. (One well-known base in the former Howard Street Mill in West Belfast is heavily fortified, and its occupants call it 'The Submarine' because it lacks windows.) Often small sub-units are detached to border PVCPs and observation posts (OPs) for long periods. Regular foot patrols are sent out in urban and rural areas. Urban patrols last only a few hours, but in rural areas patrols can last a number of days and can involve the setting up of covert OPs covering remote border crossing points or the homes of terrorist suspects. Most of these operations are carried out by units of section size or less, and present junior non-commissioned officers with challenging tests of their leadership qualities. A high degree of traditional infantry skills are needed by soldiers on rural patrols.

Larger operations involving platoons or companies are mounted to protect EOD teams or police responding to terrorist incidents; e.g., if the police need to carry out forensic examinations at the scene of a crime or to search a house for hidden arms, then Army units provide a cordon around the area. Units manning cordons in rural areas often have to stay in position for days at a time, but in urban areas troops are rotated after a few hours. Cordon operations are not popular with the troops involved but they are very necessary. In border regions transport is normally by helicopter because of the danger to overt road movements from land mines or culvert bombs.

During their stay in Northern Ireland roulement units rarely have time to relax, and are constantly under pressure. In 'hard' Republican areas troops used to be regularly subjected to highly provocative verbal abuse or 'brickings' (stone throwing) from local people who support the PIRA. This was sometimes hard to bear with the required self-restraint: flying bricks can kill; and immediate, unrestrained, close-quarter gloating over the body of a comrade killed or maimed by a bomb or sniper could tempt soldiers to regard local women and children with some hostility. That discipline has so rarely broken down under even these circumstances is a great tribute to the special qualities of the British soldier; and during the late 1980s and early 1990s this kind of behaviour has tailed off significantly. For soldiers on their first roulement tour there is a certain excitement about them, but older soldiers tend to regard them as a bit of a chore. Troops on checkpoint or static guard duty complain of intense boredom. Soldiers find they have to deal with all the problems associated with policing, such as attending road accidents, patching-up domestic disputes, and even rescuing cats stuck up trees.... While being prepared at all times to deal with PIRA attacks, troops also have to bear in mind that the overwhelming majority of Northern Ireland's population are not gun-toting terrorists. Good relations with local people are essential to undermining support for terrorist groups.

Since the mid-1970s it has been very rare for uniformed soldiers manning PVCPs or on routine patrols to exchange fire, or have 'contacts', with armed terrorists. In the period 1976 to 1987 only nine armed terrorists were shot by uniformed soldiers. Some units can now go through a whole tour without firing a round in anger. Most

Vintage 0.50 cal. heavy machine guns were re-issued to units after a number of PVCPs were devastated by PIRA 'human bombs' in the 1990s. This example is being test fired by a Highlander. (AIS HQ NI)

1990s era patrol order. This soldier has marked his webbing strap with his blood group. Under his commercially purchased 'SAS' smock is Improved Northern Ireland Body Armour. (42 (North West) Brigade PIO)

ing a five-man patrol from the Royal Artillery (serving in an infantry role) was diverted to the scene. The patrol arrested the gunmen and seized two assault rifles, but were then confronted by a mob of 40 local people demanding the release of the terrorists. The soldiers held their ground until reinforcements arrived. Such operations are nowadays the exception rather than the rule.

Many Security Forces operations are now directed at collecting intelligence on PIRA suspects. The census first compiled in the 1970s has been constantly updated, so Army patrols know details of everybody who lives on their patch; PIRA suspects or 'players' can be closely monitored. Patrols have photo-montages of the 'players' to enable them to instantly recognise them at checkpoints; these are known to the troops as 'bingo cards'. (It was copies of such documents that were at centre of the Stevens investigation after rogue UDR soldiers passed them on to Loyalist terrorists to enable murder squads to select their victims.)

Patrols and checkpoints also have direct access to *Vengeful*, the RUC's computer which lists the registration of every motor vehicle in the province; this provides Security Forces patrols anywhere in Northern Ireland with car registration details within seven seconds. Intelligence experts are also able to cross-reference patrol reports via *Vengeful* to monitor traffic movement throughout the province. The information is used to help prosecute PIRA suspects or to plan executive action to pre-empt terrorist attacks.

It is the ultimate ambition of the Army that it should eventually be able to scale down its involvement to such an extent that the RUC does not have to call on its services at all except for specialist support, as is the case in the rest of the UK.

Rules of Engagement

Soldiers in Northern Ireland are subject to the rule of law and have no special legal protection if they kill or injure civilians in the course of their duties. The RUC investigates every incident where Security Forces action result in death or injury. On a number of occasions soldiers have been brought before civilian courts charged with murder and other offences against members of the public. In addition the Army can also take disciplinary action against soldiers who break the law.

Security Forces personnel are allowed by law to use 'reasonable force' to prevent crime or assist in the lawful arrest of offenders or suspects. This is the doctrine of 'minimum force', and its interpretation is a matter of some debate. Ultimately what is justified is up to the police or the civilian courts to decide, depending on the circumstances of the incident. This places soldiers in a difficult position

terrorist suspects are arrested in their homes or at checkpoints. The RUC must then use traditional detective skills to build a case against the suspect that will stand up in court.

Contacts now fall into two main categories: terrorist gun or bomb attacks, which are normally brief and come at the least expected time. Troops have to act quickly to catch the terrorists before they make their getaway; the terrorists are usually long gone before the Army can respond. Painstakingly slow follow-up operations then have to be carried out to secure the terrorist's firing point for forensic examination.

Snap operations are mounted when a uniformed patrol spots suspicious activity and decides to intervene before the terrorists can mount an attack. Perhaps the most famous recent incident occurred in 1990 when a Lynx helicopter pilot on a routine mission spotted a car in South Armagh containing armed men. Another helicopter carry-over whether their actions might make them subject to prosecution at a later date. In the question of the use of firearms this problem is most acute. Soldiers are issued with the famous 'Yellow Card' which states the circumstances under which soldiers can open fire. Firearms are deemed to be weapons of last resort and may only be used when life is in danger and there is no other way of preventing the danger. If it is essential to fire, only aimed shots should be fired and no more rounds should be fired than is necessary. When practicable, a warning should be given before opening fire. These rules have been the subject of considerable controversy, particularly when undercover units are involved.

Under emergency legislation the soldiers have a number of special legal powers to aid them in their duties in support of the RUC. Soldiers have the power to stop and question any person about their movements or knowledge of terrorist incidents; search any persons for unlawful possession of weapons; arrest without warrant for up to four hours any person suspected of committing an offence (after four hours the suspect must be released or re-arrested by the RUC); enter premises in the course of operations to preserve the peace; enter premises to search for unlawful weapons (specific authority is needed from a commissioned officer before dwelling houses are entered); stop vessels or vehicles to search for unlawful arms; control

A paratrooper in Belfast 1992. He is wearing commercially purchased boots and a jump helmet, with distinctive cover. This soldier has written his blood group on the side of his helmet. The Parachute Helmet can be differentiated from the Combat Helmet by the strap. (1 PARA)

restricted highways and access to buildings. The 1991 Northern Ireland (Emergency Provisions) Act created the office of Independent Assessor of Military Complaints, to scrutinise non-criminal complaints against members of the armed forces, e.g. allegations of improper behaviour by troops at checkpoints. During 1990 there were 196 formal complaints against the Army: 45 were substantiated; 84 were not; in a further 56 cases the Army denied the complaint; one case established fault by both parties; two cases are still awaiting investigation. Criminal complaints remain subject to investigation by the RUC.

N.I.T.A.T.

Prior to deployment all units, either roulement or resident, now undergo an intense training programme in the UK run by the Northern Ireland Training and Advisory Team (NITAT). Classroom training and role-playing sessions are used to brief soldiers on legal rules covering opening fire, arrest procedures, checkpoint procedures, dealing with the media, and intelligence gathering. NITAT staff make it their business to be fully up-to-date on terrorist weapons and tactics. Commanders are briefed on their

TAORs, and receive detailed intelligence on key terrorists whom they are likely to encounter. Familiarisation visits are carried out to Northern Ireland to ensure a smooth transition when units arrive in the province. The high point of the NITAT package is a series of exercises to test the practical application of all this information. Two weeks are spent on specialist urban ranges in Kent to perfect urban patrolling, marksmanship and public order tactics. Soldiers from other units are drafted in to play rioting crowds or angry members of the public. A week is then spent in Norfolk perfecting rural operations, and again a 'live' enemy is provided to add to the realism.

A wide range of specialist equipment, such as riot shields, baton or rubber bullet guns, helmets, Improved Northern Ireland Body Armour (INIBA), vehicles and communications equipment is now available to troops deploying to Northern Ireland. In the early 1970s much of this equipment was improvised, e.g. riot helmets based on converted motor cycle helmets, and off-the-shelf purchases of American M69 and M1952 flak jackets. These proved to be far from ideal. 'Pig' APCs also underwent extensive modification in an exercise called Operation 'Bracelet' to provide armour protection from 7.62mm armour-piercing rounds. So-called 'Kremlin Pigs' were fitted with wire mesh screens as protection from RPG-7 rocket rounds. 'Flying Pigs' were developed, with extending mesh screens fitted to their sides to provide protection for troops in riot situations. Land Rovers were provided with add-on Vehicle Protection Kits (VPKs). While the 'Pig' still soldiers on in many forms it is slowly being superseded by purpose-built Armoured Patrol Vehicle (APV) Land Rovers and internal security versions of the Saxon wheeled APC. Armoured Fiat-Allis bulldozers (called 'Scooby-Doos') are used by Royal Engineers units to remove barricades during riots.

On a number of occasions the Army has experimented with water cannons for riot control, using both Pyrene and Mercedes-Benz machines, but it has never been satisfied with the results. The vehicles were either too big for the narrow streets of Northern Ireland cities, or the water supply was insufficient to deal with determined rioters. After bitter experience the Security Forces have come to rely on vehicles and baton guns as their main riot control weapons. Vehicles, generally armoured Land Rovers or 'Flying Pigs', are used to set up road blocks to contain riots in

This lance-corporal from 3 PARA has a 40mm Luchaire CLAW (Close Light Assault Weapon) rocket grenade attached to his webbing. The bulge caused by his INIBA can be seen at the top of his para smock. He is also wearing German para boots rather than British issue footwear. (Cpl M. Champress, 3 PARA)

A front view of the 1990 vintage EOD suit. (Tim Ripley)

The rear of an EOD suit. (AIS HQ NI)

specific zones, and then slowly squeeze the rioters into smaller areas. Baton guns are then used to keep rioters at a safe distance. If the Security Forces need to take the offensive then lightly equipped 'snatch squads' foray from behind cover to arrest identified ringleaders.

Support units

Perhaps the most famous military units deployed in Northern Ireland are the bomb disposal or EOD teams of the **Royal Army Ordnance Corps**. They are in action on a daily basis, attempting to defuse or 'make safe' terrorist bombs and arms dumps. This task in Northern Ireland is the responsibility of 321 Explosive Ordnance Disposal (EOD) Company, RAOC. It is the only agency in the province permitted to investigate and make safe suspect improvised explosive devices (IEDs), with detachments in Londonderry, Armagh, Bessbrook, Omagh, Lisburn and Belfast. In addition to this vital task their daily contact with terrorist weaponry enables them to provide the Security Forces with continual intelligence up-dates on developments in the terrorist arsenal.

EOD teams are headed by an operator or Ammunition Technical Officer (ATO), who makes safe devices; he is assisted by a team of Ammunition Technicians (ATS), who drive the team's specialist vehicles and operate support equipment. A RAOC spokesman, in a classic case of understatement, said that EOD operators had 'to be stable-minded and technically well-qualified'. It is very rare today for EOD operators to manually make safe a device in the classic fashion made famous by World War Two 'UXB' films. Wherever possible robots known as 'wheelbarrows' are used to approach IEDs and then make them safe without the operator having to enter the danger zone of the device. If there is no alternative the operator will put on the famous armoured EOD suit before approaching the device. In urban areas EOD teams work from specially modified Mercedes-Benz or Ford Transit vans, but in rural areas their equipment has to be helicoptered to the sites of suspect devices. Specially modified all-terrain vehicles and trailers called Blackboards have been developed for this role. The current RAOC vehicles have replaced modified 'Pigs' or Saracen APCs and Goblin and Gobbler load carrying vehicles. During their operations EOD teams are very vulnerable to attack, so whenever they are called into action cordons are placed in position to protect them.

Over the past 23 years EOD teams have dealt with over 40,000 emergency calls, averaging about 40 a week. Of these calls over 4,700 were actual terrorist bombs, involving a total of some 205,000lbs of explosives. During this period 17 operators and three other team members have been killed. The largest device neutralised to date was an 8,000lb bomb in September 1991; this was in a trailer and was intended for use against a PVCP, but had become bogged down in a field while being positioned by the PIRA. During 1991 321 (EOD) Company had its busiest year since 1978 responding to 1,758 calls. Devices made safe

A 'Wheelbarrow' makes safe an IED inside a car. (AIS HQ NI)

An ATO moves in to check the scene. (AIS HQ NI)

ranged from large vehicle bombs to under-vehicle IEDs or booby traps and letter bombs. In total 6,576kg of explosives were detonated by terrorists in 1991, and 6,867kg of explosives were recovered by the Army.

In recognition of their gallantry EOD team members serving in Northern Ireland have received, by 1992, two George Crosses, 14 OBEs, 21 MBEs, 30 George Medals and 60 Queen's Gallantry Medals. The most recent award was made in 1990 when WO1 Barry Johnson was awarded the George Cross after being injured while manually defusing PIRA mortar rounds endangering a hospital.

Working closely with EOD teams are Royal Engineers search teams. It is their job to actually find suspect IEDs or arms dumps and then mark safe routes to them for the ATO. They have sniffer dogs and other equipment to enable them to detect explosives and the command wires that control IEDs. Most infantry units also have search advisors and search teams, who are trained by the Royal Engineers, to carry out these tasks if no specialist search teams are available.

The **Army Air Corps** (AAC) and **Royal Air Force** (RAF) provide invaluable air support for Security Forces

The famous 'Wheelbarrow' in close-up. Since the early versions entered service in the 1970s its design has gone through several modifications. (AIS HQ NI)

operations throughout Northern Ireland. On average the AAC flies 600 sorties a week and moves 15,000 people a month around the province. Aldergrove International Airport and the old RAF base at Ballykelly near Londonderry are the main air bases in the province. At Ballykelly, 5 Regiment AAC has 655 Squadron with Lynx AH.Mk.1s and Gazelle AH.Mk.1s for observation, casualty evacuation and troop transport work. The regiment's headquarters flight of Gazelles and Lynxes is also based at Ballykelly. At Aldergrove is 665 Squadron with Lynxes and Gazelles, and No. 1 Flight with Defender AL.Mk.1 surveillance aircraft; the fixed-wing Defenders are considered more stable platforms for air-to-ground photography than helicopters.

Since its introduction in the mid-1970s the Lynx has proved to be a superb machine for moving troops quickly around rural areas. It is often used to position mobile 'Eagle' patrols at short notice. In border areas quick reaction forces (QRFs) are held on standby at heli-ports with a Lynx ready to respond to incidents. For observation duties the Gazelle has proved very successful and a number have been fitted with specialist equipment, such as the Heli-Teli airborne video observation system, which is linked to ground control centres. When two Army corporals were murdered by a Catholic mob in 1988 after blundering into a funeral march, images from Heli-Teli were used to track down and convict those involved in the killings.

The RAF support helicopter force in Northern Ireland is based at Aldergrove and is centred on No. 230 Squadron, which flies elderly Puma HC.Mk.1 helicopters. These are augmented at regular intervals by Wessex HC.Mk.2 and Chinook HC.Mk.18 helicopters. Border Security Force bases rely on the RAF helicopters to keep them supplied. Both AAC and RAF helicopter crews use night vision goggles to give them a 24-hour capability.

A growing threat has been the reported acquisition of heat-seeking surface-to-air guided missiles by the PIRA. A number are believed to have been fired at British helicopters but no hits have been recorded, most likely because of poor operator training. To help counter this threat most helicopters operating in Northern Ireland are being fitted with electronic countermeasures and heat shrouds over engine exhausts.

The **Royal Navy** provides vital support to the Army to prevent the seaborne movement of arms and terrorists. For use in open waters two Bird Class patrol boats, HMS *Kingfisher* and HMS *Cygnet*, were deployed in Northern Ireland waters to replace vintage Ton Class minesweepers. Inshore waters such as Neagh and Carlingford Loughs are patrolled by two Loyal Class tenders, HMS *Alert* and HMS *Vigilant*. All these vessels carry detachments of Royal Marines and Rigid Raider assault boats for search operations. On a number of occasions these vessels have come under PIRA fire from the Irish Republic shore of

Left: A patrol of 1 CHESHIRE board an Army Air Corps Lynx helicopter at a South Armagh Security Forces base. (42 (North West) Brigade PIO)

A RAF Wessex helicopter lifts from the HLS at Bessbrook Mill Security Forces base in South Armagh. For most of the 1970s this was the busiest heliport in the world. (42 (North West) Brigade PIO)

Carlingford Lough. Fleet Air Arm Wessex Gazelle and Lynx helicopters have also on occasions deployed to Northern Ireland to relieve the pressure on the AAC and RAF.

Perhaps the most high profile contribution of the Senior Service to British military operations in Northern Ireland has been the role played by **Royal Marine Commando** units. Battalion-sized Commandos have regularly deployed to the province on roulement tours, and there has rarely been a year when Royal Marine Commandos have not been on duty in Northern Ireland. The operations carried out by the Royal Marines are essentially similar to those undertaken by Army units. Commandos also take turns as the Spearhead Battalion.

The **Royal Military Police** (RMP) have been heavily involved in Northern Ireland, and in the 1970s two full RMP regiments with some 900 personnel were stationed in the province. By the 1980s this commitment had been reduced to a single regiment, 1 Regiment RMP, with a headquarters and five provost companies totalling some 450 personnel. They have an important role protecting sections of Belfast city centre, providing VIP escort, and investigating criminal allegations against members of the Army. RMP Special Investigation Branch (SIB) personnel were closely involved in the Stevens inquiry into the leaking of Security Force documents by UDR soldiers to Loyalist paramilitaries.

Female soldiers of the **Women's Royal Army Corps** (WRAC) have provided vital support to Army units in Northern Ireland since the early 1970s. In addition to administration duties WRAC searchers were assigned to most infantry units to search females and children at checkpoints and during house searches. This placed them in the frontline of the conflict. By the late 1980s most infantry battalions serving in Northern Ireland were usually accompanied by a WRAC platoon. After the disbandment of the WRAC in April 1992 its soldiers were either absorbed into the regiments or corps to which they were attached or became part of the new Adjutant General's Corps.

Intelligence

From the first days of the Army's deployment in Northern Ireland it has had an insatiable appetite for intelligence information on terrorist groups. The Army's experience in colonial counter-insurgency campaigns had convinced it that only through good intelligence would the terrorists be defeated. General Sir Frank Kitson is perhaps the best-known theorist of this exacting form of warfare. In his books *Low Intensity Warfare* and *A Bunch of Fives* the general describes how he organised groups of 'turned' Mau-Mau guerrillas during the Kenyan Emergency. His so-called 'counter-gangs' infiltrated and then destroyed guerrilla organisations from the inside.

RUC Chief Constable Sir Hugh Annesley at a RUC passing out parade in 1991. He formerly served in the Metropolitan Police's anti-terrorist branch and was *appointed to the top police job in Northern Ireland in 1989 after Sir Jack Hermon's retirement. (RUC) See colour plate J1.*

Given the unique legal and political situations in Northern Ireland the lessons of colonial operations proved difficult to apply. In 1969, as a young SAS major, Peter de la Billiere (who was later to command British forces in the Middle East during the Gulf War) wrote in the *Royal United Services Institute Journal* that the British Army's recent counter–insurgency successes in the Far East should be relegated to 'the library of history'; for example, the assassination of terrorist leaders by 'turned' terrorists was certainly precluded by British law. (In January 1992 Brian Nelson, a locally reunited Army intelligence agent working inside the UDA, was jailed for his part in sectarian murders.) Intelligence operations in Northern Ireland have always had a very different character from those undertaken against foreign or colonial enemies.

Not surprisingly, this is one area where the Security Forces are unwilling to talk openly about their operations; but through a variety of sources much information has emerged. While most of the information was current when it was made public it is more than likely that the Security Forces have changed their procedures and tactics as a result of the subsequent publicity. Many media reports about undercover or covert operations are also heavily tinged with 'black propaganda': terrorist groups want to cover up their shortcomings and undermine the image of the Security Forces, while the Security Forces want to deter terrorists from further operations and sow division in their ranks by spreading rumours of betrayal.

Security Forces undercover or plain clothes operations fall into two categories: intelligence gathering, and 'executive action' to pre-empt terrorist operations. Intelligence gathering is now a highly sophisticated process, but in the early days of the Army's deployment it was a very haphazard affair. The chaotic situation on the streets and the political differences between the British Government and the Stormont regime meant that there was little overall co-ordination between the Army, MI5 and the RUC. With no intelligence coming from outside agencies Army units ended up forming their own plain clothes intelligence teams to patrol their TAORs in the hope of picking up useful information or informants. Intelligence staff at brigade level and Headquarters Northern Ireland also tried to set up their own network of agents. Not surprisingly, this situation soon resulted in chaos. On occasions plain clothes patrols shot at each other under the impression that they had run into PIRA ASUs, or were arrested by uniformed Army patrols. The PIRA's own counter–intelligence operations also became quite successful at 'blowing' the Army's amateurish undercover squads. Perhaps the most famous incident was the 'Four Square Laundry affair' in 1972 when an Army undercover team was discovered by the PIRA and had to fight its way out, one soldier being killed. After much trial and error a proper system for the collection and dissemination of intelligence on terrorist groups was eventually established by the RUC, Army Intelligence and MI5.

A wide variety of sources are used. Patrol reports and other information from uniformed soldiers and policemen out on the streets are very important, enabling the movements of known suspects to be monitored. A series of confidential phone lines enable members of the public to pass information to the Security Forces, and these have often been used by disgruntled members of terrorist organisations to settle private scores. Agents and informers recruited by Army Intelligence, RUC Special Branch and MI5 to work inside terrorist groups are often a source of high grade intelligence obtained at great risk.

The 'Stalker affair' revealed that the Security Forces are increasingly using electronic eavesdropping equipment to track terrorists and 'bug' arms caches. Covert observation posts are established by Army units to keep border crossing points or the homes of suspects under round-the-clock surveillance. The RUC, MI5 and Army all have units to carry out this type of operation; in the case of the Army, unconfirmed press reports suggest that its title is 14 Intelligence and Security Company. The unit's existence came to light after two controversial incidents in Belfast. In September 1989 one team shot dead a Loyalist killer making his escape on a motorcycle from the scene of a sectarian murder. In January 1990 three robbers were shot by under-

1: Cpl., 1st Bn., Parachute Regt.; 1972
2: Royal Marine Driver, 45 Commando; 1971
3: Pte., 2nd Bn., Queen's Regt.; 1969

A

1: Gunner, 7th Regt., Royal Artillery; 1977
2: Pte., 1st Bn., Duke of Edinburgh's
   Royal Regt.; 1985
3: Pte., 1st Bn., Black Watch; 1978

B

C

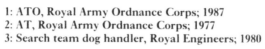

1: ATO, Royal Army Ordnance Corps; 1987
2: AT, Royal Army Ordnance Corps; 1977
3: Search team dog handler, Royal Engineers; 1980

D

1: Pte., Ulster Defence Regt.; 1971
2: Greenfinch, Ulster Defence Regt.; 1989
3: Pte., Ulster Defence Regt.; 1988

E

1: Constable, Royal Ulster Constabulary; 1989
2: Constable, Royal Ulster Constabulary; 1987
3: Constable, DMSU, Royal Ulster
   Constabulary; 1984

F

1: Pte., 1st Bn., Cheshire Regt.; 1991
2: Pte., 2nd Bn., Queen's Regt.; 1990
3: Pte., 3rd Bn., Light Infantry; 1992

G

1: Constable, Special Branch,
   Garda Siochana; 1984
2: Sgt., Irish Army; 1988
3: Pte., Army Ranger Wing; 1987
4: Leading Seaman, Irish Naval
   Service; 1985

H

1: Pte., 1st Bn., Royal Green Jackets; 1969
2: Sgt., 1st Bn., King's Own Royal
   Border Regt.; 1976
3: Pte., 1st Bn., King's Regt.; 1972

1: RUC Chief Constable, Sir Hugh Annersley; 1990
2: Lt. Gen., British Army; 1970
3: Maj., 1st Bn., Royal Green Jackets; 1974

J

1: Sgt., 1st Bn., Parachute Regt.; 1989
2: Pte., 1st Bn., King's Own Scottish
    Border Regt.; 1990
3: Pte., 1st Bn., Cheshire Regt.; 1991

1: Capt., Army Air Corps; 1990
2: Staff Sgt., Royal Electrical and Mechanical Engineers; 1987
3: Loadmaster, Royal Air Force; 1980

cover soldiers while holding up a Belfast betting shop; it turned out that the three were petty criminals armed with imitation weapons. In both cases the soldiers are believed to have been on routine surveillance when they chanced upon the incidents.

According to Mark Urban's recent book on covert operations in Northern Ireland (*Big Boy's Rules*, Faber & Faber, London, 1992), intelligence pointing to terrorist operations is passed up the chain of command to the joint RUC/Army Tasking and Co-ordination Groups in each RUC Region/Army Brigade. Decisions are then made on how to respond. Arms caches, for example, can simply be seized, the suspects arrested, or protection increased around intended targets. Sometimes operations are allowed to continue with the intention of catching the terrorists red handed. Specially trained units are then called in to carry out executive action to thwart the terrorist operation.

The Special Air Service

The SAS first served in Northern Ireland in 1969 when D Squadron of 22 SAS operated openly in County Down to try to intercept Protestant gun-runners. Until 1976 individual members are believed to have served in intelligence posts throughout the Province to try and bring order to the chaos reigning in these organisations at the time. Amid much publicity in January 1976 'a squadron' of the SAS was sent to South Armagh after the killing of 21 civilians by PIRA, and the deaths of three soldiers when their observation post was overrun by PIRA. The Army orchestrated a spate of lurid press articles to cultivate the SAS's 'bogeyman' image with the intention of scaring the PIRA back across the border. On the ground the SAS element set up a series of covert observation posts to keep terrorist suspects under round-the-clock surveillance. In 1978 the SAS element on duty in Northern Ireland started to operate throughout the province. As the Security Forces' covert surveillance capability improved the SAS were able to reduce their involvement, and began to be used almost exclusively for executive action. By the end of the 1980s the SAS presence in Northern Ireland had been reduced to a single troop made up of specially selected members of the Regiment.

SAS teams have been involved in a number of dramatic ambushes of PIRA ASUs; between 1976 and 1987 25 PIRA members were killed in ambushes. By comparison, in the same period uniformed troops killed only nine PIRA men. In the most spectacular SAS ambush to date eight PIRA men were killed while they were trying to blow up Loughgall Police Station in May 1987. The most recent SAS ambush occurred in February 1992 when four PIRA men were killed and another two captured as they were about to attack a police station at Coalisland with a 12.7mm heavy machine gun mounted on a truck.

Plain clothes Security Forces personnel are governed by the same legal rules for the use of force as uniformed troops. The RUC investigate all such incidents, and on occasions members of the SAS have had to answer to murder

RUC officers and a RMP NCO on patrol in Belfast. The Military Policeman is wearing 58 pattern webbing without kidney pouches. (RUC)

charges; they were found not guilty. In ambush situations involving heavily armed groups of terrorists the possibility of giving warnings or making arrests without the Security Forces suffering heavy casualties is almost non-existent. 'Shooting to wound' is not a viable option given the ability of terrorists to keep on shooting or to detonate explosives even when injured. It is now common after this type of incident for the PIRA and their political supporters to claim that Security Forces are operating a 'shoot-to-kill' policy, i.e. killing PIRA suspects out of hand rather than attempting to arrest them. This is a classic case of the PIRA starting to believe its own propaganda.

THE ULSTER DEFENCE REGIMENT

Since the late 1970s the British Government has increasingly relied on locally recruited units to enable the Regular Army to scale down its involvement. While the RUC has been in the forefront of this effort, the Army also devoted considerable resources to improving the effectiveness of the UDR. By 1990 the Regiment was providing military support for the RUC in 80 per cent of Northern Ireland.

The UDR has had a turbulent history. It has suffered the highest casualties of any Army regiment that has served in Northern Ireland, and has also been embroiled in heated political controversy. In July 1992 the UDR was merged with the Regular Army battalions of the Royal Irish Rangers (traditionally recruited in both the UK and the Irish Republic) to form the Royal Irish Regiment — presumably with the aim of removing, over time, the main reasons for this controversial image.

The UDR was formed in 1970 after the disbandment of the Ulster Special Constabulary or 'B Specials', discredited by their involvement in sectarian violence during the riots of 1969. By forming the UDR as a regiment of the British Army recruiting from both Catholic and Protestant communities it was hoped to create a force that would bridge the sectarian divide. In the first year some 18 per cent of its soldiers were Catholic; but within a few months most had left because of intimidation either by the PIRA or Loyalist paramilitaries.

At its peak in 1972 the UDR had 11 battalions spread throughout Northern Ireland. It included some 8,345 part-time soldiers — 95 per cent of its strength — in 1972; but by the 1990s this had stabilised at 3,000 part-timers, 3,000 permanent cadre soldiers, and 140 attached Regular Army soldiers in key command and training posts. Battalion organisations were altered at regular intervals to reflect recruiting trends and the tactical situation on the ground. In the Regiment's final form it boasted seven battalions: 1st/9th (County Antrim), 2nd/11th (County Armagh), 3rd (County Down), 4th/6th (County Fermanagh & County Tyrone), 5th (County Londonderry), 7th/11th

A joint RUC/Army rural VCP in South Armagh. The RUC constable is wearing Army issue combat high boots and has a 7.62mm Self-Loading Rifle slung over his shoulder. (42 (North West) Brigade PIO)

A joint UDR/RUC VCP in Belfast city centre during the mid-1980s. The Land Rover has been fitted with a Vehicle Protection Kit, including a 'wire cutter' post. (AIS HQ NI)

(City of Belfast) and 8th (County Tyrone) Battalions. Regimental headquarters was at Lisburn.

UDR units were employed on foot and vehicle patrols, VCPs, searches, static guards and command post work. They are not employed on riot control or plain clothes intelligence gathering duties; and are also kept well away from the 'hard' Republican areas of West Belfast and Londonderry. From 1975 UDR battalion headquarters began to take over command of specific Tactical Areas of Responsibility (TAORs) and often had Regular Army units placed under their command while UDR sub-units would at times be assigned to Regular Army TAORs. Each battalion had a number of platoons or companies of permanent cadre UDR troops available to it; these were for all intents and purposes the equivalent of Regular Army troops and were used as such. At weekends and evenings the part-timers were used to fill in for them. Often part-timers would finish work and then spend a night on patrol before returning to their civilian job. By the late 1980s part-timers were serving on average 12 duties a month, with some 200 UDR soldiers being deployed each evening. During periods of increased terrorist activity whole UDR battalions were called up for full-time duty; the most recent occasion was in January 1992 after the PIRA bombing

offensive against Belfast city centre when three battalions were called up.

By 1991 UDR units were equipped with standard British Army weapons and signals equipment, including some 5,843 SA-80 rifles and 912 Light Support Weapons; in addition the Regiment held 167 L67 riot guns. More than 2,000 9mm Browning and Walther handguns were used by the UDR, of which almost two-thirds were issued as personal protection weapons to off-duty soldiers. Some 50 Shortland armoured cars were also in service alongside over 400 armoured and Land Rovers. The majority of these had been modified with Armoured Protection Kits (APKs), although specialist Armoured Patrol Vehicle (APV) versions of the Land Rover were also in service.

Permanent cadre soldiers were trained to Regular Army standard, and officers were sent to the Royal Military Academy Sandhurst for training. Part-timers and permanent cadre soldiers were trained at the UDR depot at Ballykinler, although the latter spent nine weeks on their basic training course. Part-timers had to complete an

The first armoured Land Rover to enter service with the RUC was known as the Hotspur, is an up-armoured version of the Series III vehicle. (Bob Morrison/Military Scene)

eight-day basic training course and at least 12 days training each year. Terms of service for permanent cadre soldiers were no different from those of the Regular Army except that they were only obliged to serve in Northern Ireland.

Since 1973 the UDR fielded women soldiers, who were universally known as 'Greenfinches' after their original radio callsign. The 475 part-time and 248 permanent cadre Greenfinches had an important role to play searching females at checkpoints, as radio operators and in administrative posts.

Because UDR soldiers lived in the community they fulfilled an important secondary role of picking up intelligence on terrorist activity, this being particularly true of part-timers whose civilian jobs regularly took them into rural areas difficult for uniformed Security Force patrols to monitor. Unfortunately this made UDR soldiers very vulnerable to terrorist attack; and some 155 of the 244 fatal casualties suffered by the UDR up until 1992 have occurred while soldiers were off-duty. A further 47 were killed after they had left the Regiment. The gallantry of the Regiment was recognised over the years with 953 honours and awards to its soldiers and Greenfinches. These include 12 Queen's Gallantry Medals, two Military Medals, 88 BEMs, 108 OBEs and 276 Mentioned in Dispatches.

Republican groups, Northern Ireland Catholic and southern Irish politicians regularly accused the UDR, particularly its part-timers, of harassing Catholics at checkpoints. Most of these accusations were never substantiated. Accusations linking a small number of UDR soldiers with Loyalist terrorist groups have been substantiated, however. Up until 1979 five UDR soldiers were convicted of murder, five for manslaughter, ten for arms and explosives offences, four for serious assaults and another nine for other terrorist

type offences. Between 1970 and 1992 seven UDR soldiers were convicted of murder, 12 of the 15 victims being Catholics suspected of terrist links. The most serious incident occurred following the killing of Laughlin 'Locky' Maginn in August 1989 by a Loyalist murder squad. After an investigation by the Deputy Chief Constable of Cambridgeshire, John Stevens, it emerged that some UDR soldiers had been systematically passing Security Forces intelligence documents on Republican suspects to Loyalist terrorists for use by murder squads.

In his report Stevens called for a major shake-up of the UDR to stop leaks of intelligence information. Recommendations included better security vetting of recruits, after it was revealed that applicants had been accepted after adverse police vetting and had later gone on to commit terrorist-related offences while in service. Strict accounting for intelligence documents was also recommended. Stevens concluded that there had been collusion between members of the UDR and illegal Loyalist groups, but stressed that 'it is restricted to a small number of individuals, who have gravely abused their positions of trust' and that it was 'not widespread or institutionalised'.

As a result of the 'Options for Change' defence cutbacks the British Ministry of Defence announced in July 1991 that the UDR would be merged with the Royal Irish Rangers in the summer of 1992. By merging the two regiments' training establishments and Regimental Headquarters it was hoped to save significant amounts of money. The new Regiment includes one general service battalion, to be part of the Regular Army and drawn largely from the Regular Army battalions of the Royal Irish Rangers. The seven home-based battalions of the new regiment are based on the old units of the UDR, and in the first few months of their existence the terms of service of former UDR part-time and permanent cadre soldiers have remained largely unchanged. It is likely that significant changes will take place as the new regiment evolves over the coming years, possibly even including the phasing out of its part-time element.

A common uniform and cap badge have been adopted by all soldiers of the new regiment. Recruits to home-based battalions will continue to train at Ballykinler. The link with the Regular Army will allow improved opportunities for soldiers and officers in the home-based battalions to travel and attend training courses and Regular Army establishments, and an improved structure of career opportunities.

IRISH SECURITY FORCES

The *Garda Siochana* (Irish Police) and the Irish Defence Forces make an important contribution to the continuing campaign against terrorism in Ireland, particularly targeting the PIRA and the INLA. On a number of occasions since the Irish Civil War in the early 1920s the Irish Government has had to contend with regular challenges to its authority by extreme Republican groups who regard it as 'collaborating' with the British for accepting the partition of Ireland. Stern measures, including internment without trial, were used to contain these activities.

The conflict in Northern Ireland has proved to be a great test of the Irish Security Forces. During the tense months of July and August 1969 Irish troops were deployed to the border with Northern Ireland. Officially they were there to set up field hospitals and refugee camps for Catholics who might be driven south by Protestant mobs; however, some sources suggest that they were prepared to intervene if the 'Doomsday' scenario of outright civil war developed. The arrival of British troops on the streets of Belfast and Londonderry stabilised the situation, however.

With the launching of the PIRA offensive in 1970 the emphasis of Irish Security Forces operations changed considerably. Draconian laws were enacted to ban Sinn Fein representatives from appearing on Irish television and radio. Heavy sentences are handed out to PIRA and INLA terrorists convicted in Irish courts. Co-operation with the Security Forces in Britain and Northern Ireland has at times been strained because of legal problems over the extradition of terrorist suspects from the Republic. The 1985 Anglo-Irish Agreement smoothed many of these problems, but they have not been completely resolved. It is understood that intelligence co-operation between the Irish Special Branch and their counterparts in Belfast and London is very good.

The 11,000 strong Garda Siochana is a largely unarmed force, except for elite Special Branch units which have on occasion engaged in gun battles with Republican terrorists. The brunt of the Irish Government's operations against terrorism have therefore fallen on the Irish Defence Forces. A considerable part of the Irish Defence Budget is devoted to internal security operations. Three Irish Army

To replace the Hotspur the RUC started to acquire up-armoured versions of the One-Ten Land Rover, called the Tangi. (Bob Morrison/Military Scene)

infantry battalions and a cavalry (armoured car) squadron are deployed along the border to help the Garda; they work in close co-operation with the police and can only mount operations at the specific request of a police officer of the rank of inspector or above. Each year the units on the border mount thousands of patrols and checkpoints to counter terrorist activity. Huge quantities of arms and explosives have been discovered in search operations, including a 4,000lb bomb discovered in Donegal in March 1992. Direct links between the Garda and the RUC enable joint British–Irish security operations to be co-ordinated; e.g., if the British Army is carrying out building work on a border checkpoint, then Irish troops will be deployed on the south side of the border to complete the security cordon round the installation.

Eastern Command Infantry Force has 27 and 28 Infantry Battalions based at Dundalk and Cavan respectively. Air support is available from the Army Co-op Squadron of the Irish Air Corps based at Gormanston Aerodrome, with Cessna FR-172 light observation aircraft; Allouette III helicopters of the Army Support Squadron fly air surveillance, liaison and other missions from forward bases at Finner Camp in Donegal and Monaghan Barracks. Covering the County Donegal section of the border is 28 Infantry Battalion based at Donegal and 4 Cavalry Squadron at Longford. A number of new Army bases have been built in the border region to accommodate this force on a permanent basis. Other Army units throughout Ireland are often called upon to help the Garda carry out arms searches, the

protection of VIPs, and explosives, prisoner and cash escort duty.

In 1980 the Army Ranger Wing (ARW) was set up to give the Irish Defence Forces a special forces capability, including VIP protection, anti-hijack duties and hostage release. Personnel have been trained by the US Army Rangers, in France and in Holland. Its headquarters is at Curragh Camp, County Kildare. Due to its specialist role the ARW reports direct to the Army Chief of Staff.

Ireland's Naval Service has scored a number of successes against PIRA gun-running ships over the years. In 1984 some seven tons of arms were seized when the trawler *Marita Ann* was intercepted off County Kerry by the LE *Eithene*; this 1,800-tonne patrol vessel is the flagship of the Irish Naval Service and can embark an SA-365 Dauphin helicopter. Other ships in the Irish fleet include three *Emer* class minesweepers, a *Deirdre* class patrol vessel, and two coastal patrol vessels purchased from Britain in 1989. The main shore base is at Cork, although ships regularly operate from other Irish ports; naval headquarters are in Parkgate Street, Dublin.

Each of the 11 infantry battalions normally musters just over 600 men, all long service professional soldiers. The FN 7.62mm rifle or Gustav 9mm sub-machine gun are the standard infantry weapons; it is planned to replace them with the Austrian-designed Steyr AUG A1 5.56mm weapon. Crew-served weapons deployed with infantry battalions include the FN 7.62mm GPMG at section and platoon level; the 84mm Carl Gustav anti-tank weapon; the

Perhaps the definitive RUC armoured Land Rover is the Simba, which started to enter large scale service in the late 1980s. (Bob Morrison/Military Scene)

60mm mortar and GPMG (SF) at company level; the 90mm Bofors recoilless anti-tank rifle, 81mm mortar, .50 cal. HMG and Milan anti-tank missile at battalion level. Each infantry battalion has enough French-made Panhard M3VTT armoured personnel carriers to lift one company at a time. (Irish units have regularly been deployed to the Lebanon as part of the United Nations peacekeeping force.)

Irish cavalry units boast a wide range of armoured vehicles, including British-made Scorpion light tanks, French Panhard AML-90 and AML-60 armoured cars, Panhard M3VTT and Irish-made Timoney Mk V/VI armoured personnel carriers. Cavalry units deployed to assist the civil power generally use APCs to carry troops for use at checkpoints or to act as escorts.

With only some 13,000 men under arms and 15,000 reservists the Irish Defence Forces are considerably stretched by the need to deploy a large percentage of their forces along the 280-mile border with Northern Ireland. Its extent, and the difficult nature of the terrain, make it practically impossible for the Irish forces to totally seal the frontier. The Irish are, however, justifiably proud of their contribution to the fight against terrorism.

Irish infantrymen wearing M1952 flak jackets. The APC is a Panhard M3VTT, which is used by infantry battalions and 4 Cavalry Squadron. (Bob Morrison/ Military Scene)

THE PLATES

A1: Corporal 1st Battalion, The Parachute Regiment, 1972

While on urban patrol and riot duties Parachute Regiment soldiers in the early 1970s carried the minimal amount of kit, allowing them to debus quickly from cramped Pig APCs without snagging bulky 58 pattern webbing. Since they usually operated from nearby Army bases there was little requirement for all the personal equipment usually carried in webbing. So this soldier has stripped down his 58 pattern webbing, leaving only a water bottle and two ammo pouches. He is carrying a 7.62mm SLR, the standard British Army weapon until the late 1980s. Early Northern Ireland tours were the last time Parachute Regiment battalions wore in action the famous 'Denison' smock so beloved by the Airborne Forces. In the late 1970s it was

A line-up of Irish Defence Force personnel; note infantryman armed with the Steyr AUG A1 5.56mm weapon system. (Irish Defence Forces)

replaced by a Disruptive Pattern Material (DPM) Para smock. All Parachute Regiment soldiers sport 'DZ flashes' on their smocks to indicate their parent battalion.

A2: Royal Marine Driver, 45 Commando, 1971

While officially not part of the British Army, Royal Marine Commandos are equipped largely with uniforms, equipment and weapons similar to their Army counterparts. The exception to this of course is the famous Royal Marine Commando Green Beret and the shoulder flash worn on woollen jerseys. This 'Royal' sports typical 1960s vintage olive drab trousers and DMS boots. As in the Army, Royal Marine specialists such as drivers, radio operators and headquarters personnel regularly carried the 9mm

L3/4A1 SMG. The olive drab waterproof smock was a common item in the 1970s and early 1980s until replaced by DPM waterproof clothing. Because of the noise such clothing makes while moving through woods it is hardly ever worn during rural patrols, but is restricted to use by static guards or urban patrols.

A3: Private, 2nd Battalion, The Queen's Regiment, 1969

The first infantrymen to deploy on the streets of Ulster were dressed in a quaint mix of uniform and equipment dating from the recent and distant past. The 'Queensman's' 1944 pattern helmet or 'tin-pot' originates from a design that dated from the First World War. The DMS boots and puttees dated from the 1950s, the olive drab combat jacket and trousers were issued on a large scale in the 1960s after the British Army finally consigned its

World War Two vintage 'battledress' to history. Within a matter of months troops serving in Northern Ireland would be wearing DPM combat jackets and trousers. The 7.62mm SLR entered service in the late 1950s. In line with the Army's early peacekeeping role, troops were expected to present a 'smart soldierly' appearance even in the midst of riots. So shirts had to be pressed and ties worn and camouflage cream was never applied.

B1: Gunner, 7th Regiment Royal Artillery, 1977

This Royal Horse Artillery gunner sports uniform and equipment typical of soldiers serving in urban areas of Northern Ireland during the 1970s. He is wearing DMS boots with puttees, light weight trousers and carries a 7.62mm SLR. The American M1952 'flak jacket' was a standard item throughout the 1970s and came with a variety of covers. Some did not have collars and others had special shoulder pads to improve weapon handling. A parachute helmet and baton are carried in case a riot should develop. Recruiting problems in the late 1970s resulted in non-infantry regiments or corps such as the Royal Artillery, Royal Signals and Royal Armoured Corps, being called upon to provide manpower for service in Northern Ireland. Prior to deployment they went through the same NITAT training package as infantrymen. The defence cuts in the 1990s have again resulted in an increasing number of non-infantry units being deployed in Northern Ireland.

B2: Private, 1st Battalion, The Duke of Edinburgh's Royal Regiment, 1985

On VCP duty it is common for soldiers to carry only sidearms, usually a 9mm Browning pistol, as in this case. While fully armed and equipped colleagues stand guard, a lightly equipped searcher questions motorists and searches under cars or inside engine compartments without having to place his weapon on the ground where it may be seized in a struggle. The sidearm is secured by a Lanyard in case an attempt is made to seize it. The soldier has modified his DPM combat jacket by adding woollen cuffs. He has also sewn seams into his lightweight trousers to cut down on the amount of ironing he has to do.

B3: Private, 1st Battalion, The Black Watch, 1978

During the late 1970s the British Army started to introduce several pieces of personal equipment designed speci-

ally for use in Northern Ireland. Among the first of these was the Northern Ireland Combat Helmet, which was made of glass reinforced plastic. It featured a four-point chin strap and anchor points for Makrolon moveable visors. Units in urban areas tended to use it without a camouflage cover, while in rural areas a DPM cover was standard. This helmet was the direct predecessor to the current Combat Helmet now in standard use with the British Army. The easiest way to differentiate between the two designs is the chin strap design and cloth DPM cover — on the newer model there are elastic straps to attach foliage. Padded black leather Northern Ireland gloves and Northern Ireland patrol boots also made their first appearance in this period. The NI patrol boots were the direct predecessor of the current Combat High Boot, which replaced the very unsatisfactory DMS boot after the Falklands War.

C1: Corporal, Royal Military Police, 1971

In the first years of 'the Troubles' Royal Military Policemen continued to wear their distinctive 'Red Cap' in recognition of their unique role as soldiers with the 'power

41 Commando RM was one of the first British units to arrive in Ulster during 1969 and at first enjoyed good relations with local people, as illustrated by this photograph. (Royal Marines Museum)

of constables'. They were largely deployed in city centre areas, supporting RUC patrols or manning pedestrian entry points through security gates, designed to seal off commercial areas from terrorist bombers. Due to the confined nature of these areas M1952 'flak jackets' were standard and the 9mm L34A1 SMG was the RMP personal weapon, along with 9mm Browning pistols. This military policeman is wearing standard issue DPM combat jacket and trousers.

C2: Private, Women's Royal Army Corps searcher, Royal Military Police, 1991

Until the abolition of the Women's Royal Army Corps (WRAC) in April 1992 the British Army's women soldiers had their own distinctive regimental uniform. Henceforth a new system of uniforms based on their parent regiment or corps will be introduced. While the uniforms have been

CS gas in use during a riot in the early years of 'the Troubles'. (Airborne Forces Museum)

replaced the jobs carried out by women soldiers in Northern Ireland are largely unchanged. Members of the WRAC have served as military policewomen in RMP Provost Companies throughout 'the Troubles'. This WRAC searcher sports the final version of the WRAC military policewoman barrack dress uniform skirt, jumper and cap. When on duty outside Security Force bases M1952 flak jackets are standard. No arms are carried by women soldiers in Northern Ireland. In rural areas DPM combat kit, boots and berets are worn.

C3: Women Police Constable, Royal Ulster Constabulary, 1990

The need to provide female searchers has resulted in RUC Women Police Constables regularly working with RMP patrols in city centre areas. Like women soldiers they are unarmed. RUC WPCs wear a distinctive cap, which is unique among British police forces. This WPC is wearing Bristol body armour over her working dress uniform.

C4: Corporal, Royal Military Police, 1990

With the introduction of the SA-80 and new Combat Helmet in the mid-1980s RMP units in Northern Ireland

started to change their patrol dress. Except for the distinctive MP armband they patrol in similar combat uniforms to those worn by infantry units.

D1: Ammunition Technical Officer, Royal Army Ordnance Corps, 1987

Since RAOC ATOs or operators started making safe terrorist bombs in the early 1970s a wide range of specialist equipment has been developed to make their job considerably safer. One such item is the armoured EOD suit. Over the years it has gone through an evolutionary process that has resulted in the current version featuring a new helmet with a de-mister built into it to keep the face visor clear. The EOD suit is intended to protect all the ATO's vital organs with glass-reinforced plastic armour plates and Kevlar. It is very cumbersome to use, but has proved effective on a number of occasions when IEDs and unstable ammunition have exploded while ATOs have been trying to make them safe. When large explosive devices are involved the EOD suit is considered to have a very limited utility. ATOs are usually captains or senior warrant officers.

D2: Corporal, Ammunition Technician, Royal Army Ordnance Corps, 1977

ATOs work as a team with ATs, who help the ATO get into his EOD suit and prepare the 'Wheelbarrow' for action. If the ATO goes forward to make a device safe manually the AT monitors his progress through the 'Wheelbarrow's' video system. Because of their role ATs have to be free to climb in and out of cramped EOD vehicles so minimal personal equipment is carried. This AT is wearing barrack dress trousers with black shoes and a M1952 flak jacket. ATs are usually corporals; most eventually progress the ranks to become fully fledged ATOs.

D3: Corporal, search team dog handler, Royal Engineers, 1980

Sniffer dogs have proved invaluable in the hunt for hidden arms and explosives. Labradors are the most common breed of dog used by the Royal Engineers: more aggressive Alsatians are reserved for guard duty. The Wellington

A patrol of 1 CHESHIRE prepare to move out of a Security Forces base in South Armagh in 1991. (42 (North West) Brigade PIO)

1 PARA rural patrol kit. 1: sleeping bag 2: waterproof bergen bag 3: towel, washing & shaving kit 4: gortex waterproof jacket 5: parachute smock 6: shirt 7: boots 8: heavy wool jumper 10: socks 11: foot powder 12: face veil 13: PLCE bergen 14: sleeping rool mat 15: shovel and sandbag 16: bergen cover 17: 24hr rations 18: metal mug 19: radio and spare batteries 20: two water bottles 21: lightweight poncho 22: map and note book 23: first aid kit 24: plastic bag and white tape 25: 30 metres string 26: 4 x magazines 27: right angle torch 28: webbing.
(1 PARA)

A paratrooper fully kitted out for a rural patrol. (1 PARA)

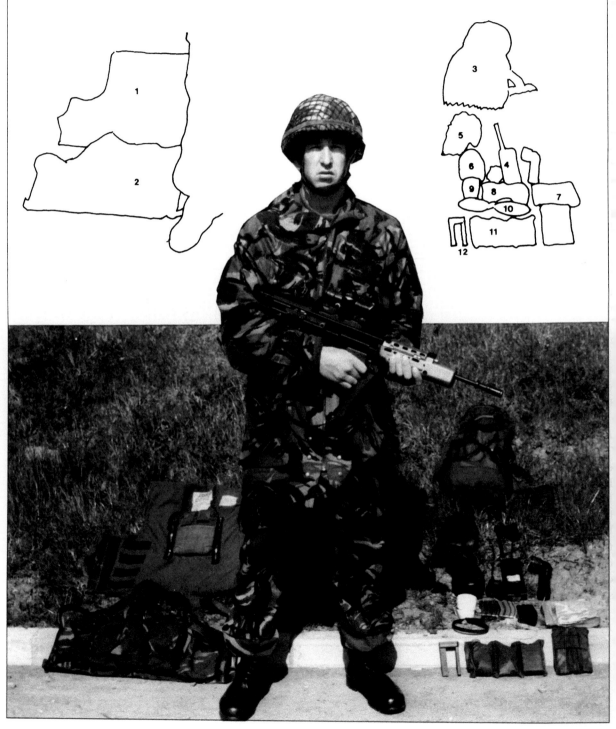

1 PARA urban patrol kit, circa 1992. 1: INIDA vest, front and rear plates 2: chest webbing 3: day sack 4: radio and spare battery 5: NI gloves 6: water bottle 7: map and notebook 8: 4 x magazines 9: white mine tape 10: restraining straps 11: first aid kit 12: magazine filler. (1 PARA)

boots date this figure to the period before the introduction of combat high boots. DMS boots were notorious for their ability to let in water, so this Sapper has adopted more practical footwear for search tasks which often have to be carried out in drains, streams and Irish bogs. Flak jackets and glass-reinforced-plastic (GRP) helmets are often worn to combat the danger of booby traps. Search teams only operate when they are protected by infantry cordons, so sidearms are carried as personal protection weapons, in this case a 9mm Browning pistol. This Sapper's DPM combat clothing consists of standard issue items.

E1: Private, Ulster Defence Regiment, 1971

In the early days few modern uniforms and little equipment were available to the UDR. Its first rifles were .303 Lee Enfields, while olive drab smocks and trousers made up the first uniforms. By 1972 7.62mm SLRs and DPM combat uniforms were in widespread use. This UDR soldier is prepared to go on VCP duty, with stripped down 58 pattern webbing to ease debussing from cramped Land Rovers.

E2: Female Private, Ulster Defence Regiment, 1989

To search females and children at VCPs the UDR recruited its first female soldiers in 1973; their original radio call-sign was 'Greenfinch' and the name has stuck. They were not members of the WRAC but fully fledged members of the UDR. This predated the Regular Army's 1992 change of policy regarding woman soldiers by some 19 years. While out on patrol in rural areas Greenfinches wear standard DPM combat kit, 58 pattern belt and the UDR beret. They are unarmed.

E3: Private, Ulster Defence Regiment, 1988

The UDR was the first non-NATO roled unit to be equipped with the SA-80 small arms system. Standard British infantry uniforms and equipment are issued to the UDR and it is now difficult to differentiate between members of the regiment and their Regular Army counterparts. UDR soldiers wear a shoulder slide, however, which has the number of their parent regiment (i.e. 4 UDR) embroidered in black. By 1992 all UDR battalions had been equipped with the 90 Pat (Inf) Equipment webbing system.

F1: Constable, Royal Ulster Constabulary, 1989

This uniform is now standard for RUC constables engaged on routine duties. The RUC issues a distinctive pale green shirt to its officers, and unlike mainland police forces all its male officers are armed at all times. Bristol body-armour is now standard issue when patrolling urban areas. This Constable also carries a Ruger pistol.

F2: Constable, Royal Ulster Constabulary, 1987

It is increasingly common for RUC officers to accompany almost all Army patrols in Northern Ireland. In rural areas the uniform in Plate F1 is impractical so RUC officers on rural patrols use equipment similar to the Army. This officer is wearing Army issue combat high boots, has ammo pouches on his belt and carries a rucksack. His M1 Carbine

A paratrooper sports typical urban patrol kit, circa 1992, including commercially purchased webbing. (1 PARA)

is fitted with a SUIT sight. During inclement weather a black hoodless waterproof jacket is worn by RUC officers on rural patrol duty.

F3: Divisional Mobile Support Unit Constable, Royal Ulster Constabulary, 1984

Divisional Mobile Support Units (formerly Special Patrol Groups) are the RUC's elite riot squads. They are deployed to police para-military funerals, political demonstrations and other potentially volatile situations. Where possible, as is the case here, they are dressed like ordinary constables, but they have riot equipment at their disposal. This includes Webley-Schermuly Anti-Riot guns which fire plastic baton rounds. Standard RUC body armour is worn, along with versions of the Army's GRP helmet.

G1: Private, 1st Battalion, The Cheshire Regiment, 1991

By late 1989 most infantry soldiers serving in Northern Ireland had been issued with the new 90 Pat (Inf) Equipment webbing designed to be used in conjunction with the SA-80 small arms system. This soldier also has commer

A GPMG gunner from 3 PARA on patrol during the summer of 1992. Note the DIY repairs to this paratrooper's combat trousers. (Cpl M. Champress, 3 PARA)

cially purchased chest webbing with a map case tucked underneath. Strapped next to the webbing is a PRC-349 radio. Many soldiers have found the 1980s issue combat clothing to be of very poor quality, and so acquire non-standard kit such as Para smocks and Norwegian shirts. Improved Northern Ireland Body Armour is worn under combat jackets. In the future the Army intends to produce the 90 Pat (Inf) Equipment webbing in DPM.

G2: Private, 2nd Battalion, The Queen's Regiment, 1990

For static guard duty in PVCPs, observation towers or guard sangars at Security Forces bases, soldiers wear body armour to protect themselves from snipers. Improved Northern Ireland Body Armour is made of composite materials and is said to be able to withstand AK-47 fire at close range. It replaced the American-made flak jackets used in the 1970s and 1980s. They used Kevlar but lost much of their ballistic protective qualities when wet. Fixing points for visors are a standard feature of the new Combat Helmet.

G3: Private, 3 Light Infantry, 1992

Troops on vehicle patrol duty in urban areas adopt a very light scale of equipment; webbing proves more of a hindrance than a help in situations where quick responses are needed. This soldier wears 1980s pattern lightweight DPM combat kit that is easily recognisable by its baggy jacket and trouser pockets. The uniform dries quickly when wet, unlike the 1970s lined combat kit which absorbed water in vast quantities. Unfortunately the new material rips easily on barbed wire fences – a common feature in rural areas – and provides no protection against wind chill. Few soldiers wear this kit if they have any choice in the matter.

H1: Garda Siochana Special Branch, 1984

Uniformed Garda Siochana officers are unarmed, so in response to increasing PIRA activity in the Republic the Irish Government equipped elite plain clothes Special Branch units with automatic weapons. They have access to a wide range of modern weapons including Heckler & Koch MP5s and the popular 9mm Uzi sub-machine guns, as shown here. Special Branch units participate in all sensitive security operations, such as the handing over of PIRA suspects being extradited to Northern Ireland. Like this officer, they are considered snappy dressers and favour Barbour jackets and brogue shoes.

H2: Sergeant, Irish Army, 1988

The Irish Army buys its equipment from a wide range of sources, although Britain has been a main supplier in the past. This is reflected in this soldier's 58 pattern webbing and 7.62mm GPMG, both standard British Army items. The rest of the uniform is of Irish origin. On internal patrols along the Northern Ireland border American M1952 flak jackets are worn.

H3: Private, Army Ranger Wing, 1987

First formed in 1980 the Army Ranger Wing (ARW) has two main roles, long-range patrolling in conventional warfare and anti-terrorist operations such as hostage release and VIP security. As with elite units world-wide, the ARW has great freedom in the weapons and equipment it chooses to use. While rarely seen, photographs of the ARW suggest that a mix of Irish Army issue equipment and commercially available items are used, including British-made DPM bergens and a variety of webbing systems. Standard Irish Army helmets are sometimes worn but in rural operations black woollen caps are used. Weapons include shotguns for close quarter work and Heckler & Koch MP5s.

H4: Leading Seaman, Irish Naval Service, 1985

As can be seen here the Irish Naval Service uniform follows traditional naval fashion, but with appropriate Irish insignia. Working dress includes light blue waterproof clothing. Flight deck crews on the EL Eithene wear blue or yellow waistcoats over blue denim fatigues. Helmets are also colour-coded.

I1: Private, 1st Battalion, The Royal Green Jackets, 1969

The first troops to be deployed in Ulster possessed very rudimentary riot control equipment. Their only protection came from 1944 pattern helmets and primitive riot shields. CS gas was the only non-lethal riot control weapon available but was of limited use in densely populated urban areas. Colonial riot tactics involving the selective shooting of riot ringleaders were considered inappropriate for the British Isles, so the British Army had to quickly re-think its tactics for dealing with civil disorder.

I2: Sergeant, 1st Battalion, The King's Own Royal Border Regiment, 1976

By the mid-1970s British riot control equipment became more sophisticated. Perspex riot shields had been introduced along with GRP helmets with moveable visors. A number of different versions of non-lethal riot control weapons had been introduced including the L1A1 grenade launcher for firing CS gas canisters and the L67, Federal (seen here) and Webley-Schermuly baton round guns for firing rubber or plastic bullets. While these are designed to deliver a sharp non-fatal bow to rioters at ranges of up to 50 metres, fatalities have occurred. At the peak of their use in

The visor system fitted to the new Combat Helmet is clearly shown in this photograph. The visor is fitted to mounting holes in the side of the helmet. This soldier of the 1st Royal Highland Fusiliers also has an iron sight fitted to his SA-80 rather than the standard SUSAT sight. (AIS HQ NI)

the early 1970s the mortality rate reached 1 per 16,000 rounds fired. As the public order situation improved in the 1980s their use, and hence fatalities, decreased dramatically. This soldier is wearing typical 1970s kit, including DMS boots with puttees, DPM combat clothing and stripped-down 58 pattern webbing.

I3: Private, 1st Battalion, The King's Regiment, 1972

To take the offensive against rioters the British Army developed the 'snatch squad' concept. These are lightly equipped, highly agile groups of soldiers who are tasked with moving forward from behind cover to apprehend selected riot ringleaders. Speed, aggression and surprise are the key to success; if the operation goes wrong the soldiers are very exposed and have to be covered by their colleagues. As with the soldier in Plate I2 the minimum amount of equipment is worn with lightweight trousers, Northern Ireland boots and a GRP Helmet.

J1: Royal Ulster Constabulary Chief Constable, Sir Hugh Annersley, 1990

As Northern Ireland's senior police officer the RUC Chief Constable is at the centre of countering terrorism in the province. He is seen here in his full dress uniform at a passing out parade for new RUC Constables.

J2: Lieutenant-General, British Army, 1970

While visiting troops in the field British generals have a reputation for adopting highly personalised uniforms – no-one tells a general he is improperly dressed! This officer is wearing a Barbour jacket (especially popular with general officers, especially those in the cavalry), barrack dress trousers and a service dress cap with general insignia.

J3: Major, 1st Battalion, The Royal Green Jackets, 1974

Field officers, captains and majors, spend much of their time on tour in Northern Ireland manning operations rooms and command posts in Security Forces bases. This officer is wearing a typical uniform for this type of work, consisting of the standard British Army working dress woollen jersey, green shirt, lightweight trousers and boots. It is possible to differentiate officers' parent regiments from rank slides on jersey epaulettes and beret badges.

K1: Sergeant, 1st Battalion, The Parachute Regiment, 1989

In rural areas patrols have to blend into the countryside while standard fieldcraft rules apply. Camouflage cream is worn on the face and helmets are covered with foliage. Note the blackened metal version of the Parachute Regiment cap badge. Because of the poor quality of 1980s issue combat kit many soldiers purchased equipment privately; this Paratrooper boasts gaiters to keep his boots dry and a bergen. A number of units are also issued with the M16A1/M203 grenade launcher combination attached to increase their firepower.

K2: Private, 1st Battalion, The King's Own Scottish Border Regiment, 1990

Patrolling goes on 365 days a year in Northern Ireland. In the depth of winter snow suits, developed for use by ski troops in Norway, are issued. The two-piece suits are simply worn over the soldiers' normal combat kit, although in very cold weather quilted jackets and trousers are also worn. A white cover is also available for the new Combat Helmet.

K3: Private, 1st Battalion, The Cheshire Regiment, 1991

This soldier is wearing DPM waterproof clothing that is now used widely by troops on urban patrol or static guard duty. This soldier is manning a trench complex, similar to a number built in the late 1980s to protect Royal Engineers building PVCPs and observation towers in border regions and occupied for many weeks at a time. Waterproof clothing is essential for these troops due to the heavy rainfall in the region.

L1: Captain (Pilot), Army Air Corps, 1990

Army Air Corps helicopter crews no longer wear flying suits when on active service. Standard issue or personally purchased DPM uniforms are worn, as with this pilot who also wears his light blue AAC beret. Unlike the RAF, which only allows commissioned officers to become pilots, the AAC has adopted the practice of training corporals to become pilots. Officers or senior NCOs command AAC

helicopters from the left seat. Crews serve in the province on four-month roulement tours from units based in mainland Britain or Germany.

L2: Staff Sergeant, Royal Electrical and Mechanical Engineers, 1987

REMEs are responsible for keeping AAC helicopters in the air. REME Aircraft Technicians (ATs) work in Light Aid Detachments (LAD) attached to each AAC regiment and squadron. Being true 'REMFs' these rear echelon personnel have been known to acquire large collections of non-standard kit, including German panzer boots, Arctic parkas and the like. Most REME ATs are highly qualified NCOs. This S/Sgt is wearing normal working dress which consists of lightweight trousers, combat high boots and a woollen jersey.

L3: Sergeant, Loadmaster, Royal Air Force, 1980

RAF helicopters always fly with a loadmaster responsible for loading passengers and cargo. Air crews are issued with standard flying overalls, but this loadmaster is following the common RAF practice, during Army support operations, of wearing a DPM combat jacket over his flying overalls.

INDEX

Figures in **bold** refer to illustrations.